Cambridge Opera Handbooks

Benjamin Britten
The Turn of the Screw

CW00547923

Benjamin Britten
The Turn of the Screw

Edited by
PATRICIA HOWARD

Lecturer in Music
The Open University

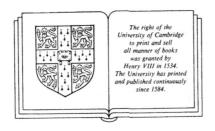

The right of the
University of Cambridge
to print and sell
all manner of books
was granted by
Henry VIII in 1534.
The University has printed
and published continuously
since 1584.

CAMBRIDGE UNIVERSITY PRESS

Cambridge
London   New York   New Rochelle
Melbourne   Sydney

PUBLISHED BY THE PRESS SYNDICATE OF THE UNIVERSITY OF CAMBRIDGE
The Pitt Building, Trumpington Street, Cambridge, United Kingdom

CAMBRIDGE UNIVERSITY PRESS
The Edinburgh Building, Cambridge CB2 2RU, UK
40 West 20th Street, New York NY 10011- 4211, USA
477 Williamstown Road, Port Melbourne, VIC 3207, Australia
Ruiz de Alarcón 13, 28014 Madrid, Spain
Dock House, The Waterfront, Cape Town 8001, South Africa

http://www.cambridge.org

First published 1985

Library of Congress catalogue card number: 84-23292

British Library Cataloguing in Publication Data

Benjamin Britten: The Turn of the Screw.
1.   Britten, Benjamin. Turn of the Screw.
1.   Howard, Patricia, 1937 –
782.1'092'4   ML410.B853

ISBN 0 521 23927 3 hardback
ISBN 0 521 28356 6 paperback

Transferred to digital printing 2004

General preface

This is a series of studies of individual operas, written for the serious opera-goer or record-collector as well as the student or scholar. Each volume has three main concerns. The first is historical: to describe the genesis of the work, its sources or its relation to literary proto- types, the collaboration between librettist and composer, and the first performance and subsequent stage history. This history is itself a record of changing attitudes towards the work, and an index of general changes of taste. The second is analytical and is grounded in a very full synopsis which considers the opera as a structure of musi- cal and dramatic effects. In most volumes there is also a musical analysis of a section of the score, showing how the music serves or makes the drama. The analysis, like the history, naturally raises questions of interpretation, and the third concern of each volume is to show how critical writing about an opera, like production and per- formance, can direct or distort appreciation of its structural ele- ments. Some conflict of interpretation is an inevitable part of this account; editors of the handbooks reflect this – by citing classic state- ments, by commissioning new essays, by taking up their own critical position. A final section gives a select bibliography, a discography and guides to other sources.

Books published

Richard Wagner: *Parsifal* by Lucy Beckett
C. W. von Gluck: *Orfeo* by Patricia Howard
W. A. Mozart: *Don Giovanni* by Julian Rushton
Igor Stravinsky: *The Rake's Progress* by Paul Griffiths
Leoš Janáček: *Kát'a Kabanová* by John Tyrrell
Benjamin Britten: *Peter Grimes* by Philip Brett
Giuseppe Verdi: *Falstaff* by James A. Hepokoski

other volumes in preparation

In affectionate and grateful memory of
Kate Flint
1913–1983

Contents

Illustrations

The illustrations are reproduced by permission, as follows: 1 and 16:
Alex von Koettlitz; 2: Anne Kirchbach; 3 and 14: Nigel Luckhurst;
4: Julian Sheppard; 5, 6 and 15: Mydtskov; 7 and 12: Angus McBean;
8 and 9: Eric Thorburn; 10 and 13: John Haynes; 11: John Piper and
The Herbert Press Ltd

Acknowledgements

I should like to thank all who have contributed to this book: my fellow authors, John Evans, Vivien Jones and Christopher Palmer, all of whom have given me valuable insights into *The Turn of the Screw*; Myfanwy Piper, who has answered vital questions which previous published sources left unanswered; Anthony Besch and Geoffrey Connor for giving their time to explain the interpretative principles behind productions which formed landmarks in the stage history of the opera; Rosamund Strode of the Britten–Pears Library; Paul Meecham of Boosey and Hawkes; the administrative staffs of Cologne Opera, English National Opera, Kent Opera, Scottish Opera and Welsh National Opera for generous help with research; The Herbert Press Ltd and Hamish Hamilton Ltd, for permission to quote from David Herbert, *The Operas of Benjamin Britten*.

Patricia Howard

September 1984

1 Henry James's 'The Turn of the Screw'

VIVIEN JONES

Readers who know nothing else about or by Henry James tend to know him as the author of *The Turn of the Screw*. This macabre tale – Rebecca West called it 'the best ghost story in the world' – has been unfailingly popular with both scholars and general readers since its publication in 1898, a rare achievement for one of James's works and unique among the difficult, experimental fiction of his later period, and as well as Britten's opera, it has inspired a play and two films. James himself is said to have been as disturbed by his tale as generations of his readers: his friend Edmund Gosse claimed that after correcting the proofs one evening James said he was 'so frightened that I was afraid to go upstairs'. But when questioned about *The Turn of the Screw* James was always evasive and dismissive. 'The thing is essentially a pot-boiler and a *jeu d'esprit*', he wrote to H. G. Wells at the end of 1898, and again, when F. W. H. Myers, a founder of the Society for Psychical Research, asked about the tale James evaded the questions: 'The *T. of the S.* is a very mechanical matter. . . rather a shameless pot-boiler.' 'Pot-boiler', certainly: *The Turn of the Screw* was written for an American weekly 'dealing in the time-honoured Christmas-tide toy' whose editors asked James for 'something seasonable', and James was glad to seize an increasingly rare opportunity for popular serial publication; '*jeu d'esprit*', perhaps, but in what sense?

James's wit is never a simple matter and it might be that this letter to Wells hints at the 'game' critics have since detected in *The Turn of the Screw*. For this is a ghost story which can undoubtedly terrify but in which the existence of the ghosts is debatable, to say the least: James's tale is in fact two tales in one; it is consistently and irresolvably ambiguous, permitting two interpretations and refusing to let the reader settle for either. Do the children 'see' the ghosts or are they the product of the governess's imagination? Are Miles and Flora preyed upon by the ghosts – or by the governess? We have no certain evi-

1

dence, for we have only her version of what happened. It is this ambiguity which has taxed and fascinated readers for at least the last sixty years, and which makes James's ghost story both a frightening tale and an examination of the imaginative mechanisms on which all ghost stories depend. It also makes *The Turn of the Screw* particularly resistant to successful adaptation, since the device of a single narrator is unavailable to drama. The playwright, or librettist, or composer brave enough to try has the choice between commitment to one interpretation and the formidable task of reproducing in another medium ambiguities which in James are so inextricably part of our experience of reading the governess's account of events at Bly.[1]

The original hint, or 'germ' as James called such ideas, for *The Turn of the Screw* is recorded in his *Notebooks* under the date 12 January 1895:

Note here the ghost-story told me at Addington. . . by the Archbishop of Canterbury: the mere vague, undetailed, faint sketch of it – being all he had been told (very badly and imperfectly), by a lady who had no art of relation, and no clearness: the story of the young children (indefinite number and age) left to the care of servants in an old country-house, through the death, presumably, of parents. The servants, wicked and depraved, corrupt and deprave the children; the children are bad, full of evil, to a sinister degree. The servants *die* (the story vague about the way of it) and their apparitions, figures, return to haunt the house *and* children, to whom they seem to beckon, whom they invite and solicit, from across dangerous places, the deep ditch of a sunk fence, etc. – so that the children may destroy themselves, lose themselves, by responding, by getting into their power. So long as the children are kept from them, they are not lost; but they try and try and try, these evil presences, to get hold of them. It is a question of the children 'coming over to where they are'. It is all obscure and imperfect, the picture, the story, but there is a suggestion of strangely gruesome effect in it. The story to be told – tolerably obviously – by an outside spectator, observer.[2]

Here at least the ghosts are real and it is their relationship with the children, with innocence, which attracts James, the governess figuring simply as a narrative technique. The idea then lay dormant for over two years until James was asked for a story by the new editor of the journal *Collier's Weekly*, who hoped to boost falling sales by offering culture for mass consumption in the form of illustrated serials by writers of James's stature. *The Turn of the Screw*, originally planned as a short story of eight to ten thousand words, grew, as James's tales had a habit of doing, to the length of a short novel and was serialised in *Collier's* in twelve episodes from January to April 1898. Unfortunately there is a gap in James's notebooks during 1897, when he was writing *The Turn of the Screw*, so we are

life persistently blunders and deviates, loses herself in the sand

denied any glimpse into the process by which Archbishop Benson's vague anecdote became the complex tale we now have. We do know, however, that James delighted in just such incomplete, half-remembered hints as starting points. They left him free to develop them according to the 'sublime economy', the logic, of art, compared with which 'life persistently blunders and deviates, loses herself in the sand' (James, *Art of the Novel*, p. 120). In other words, the actual outcome in life of relationships or situations which arrested James's attention too often, he felt, obscured their interest, dissipating the significance which the artist can isolate and emphasise. We know, too, that James had thought hard about the difficulties of the ghost story as a form and about what will really frighten a reader. In 1865, at the very beginning of his career, he had praised Wilkie Collins for 'having introduced into fiction those most mysterious of mysteries, the mysteries which are at our own doors', and he returned to the theme in 1908 in one of the Prefaces to the great New York Edition of his works, where he stressed that 'prodigies keep all their character. . . by looming through some other history – the indispensable history of somebody's *normal* relation to something'. In James, this unnerving closeness of the normal and the paranormal is brought home through the perceiving consciousness of one character: the 'human emotion and human attestation' are what 'make' the story (*Art of the Novel*, p. 256). The other vital element in James's formula for a successful ghost story is understatement. He told his heart specialist, Sir James Mackenzie, 'So long as the events are veiled the imagination will run riot and depict all sorts of horrors, but as soon as the veil is lifted, all mystery disappears and with it the sense of terror.' And in the Preface to *The Turn of the Screw* itself he again emphasises the role of the imagination:

Only make the reader's general vision of evil intense enough, I said to myself. . . and his own experience, his own imagination, his own sympathy . . . will supply him quite sufficiently with all the particulars. Make him *think* the evil, make him think of it for himself, and you are released from weak specifications.   (*Art of the Novel*, p. 176)[3]

So there are technical reasons for the ambiguity and complexity which characterise *The Turn of the Screw*, and once James had identified the figure who 'tolerably obviously' reports the tale, the logic of art demanded that an exploration of her consciousness became an intrinsic part of its interest. But for many commentators, the distance between the Archbishop's hint and James's finished version is too great to be explained simply in technical terms and vari-

role of imagination

ous additional sources – particularly for the governess – have been put forward, some more plausible than others.

For example, we can reject as highly unlikely, and unilluminating even if true, the suggestion made by one critic that Peter Quint was intended as a covert attack on George Bernard Shaw! It is much more interesting to note that, through friends and through his brother William James, the psychologist and philosopher, James was associated with the Society for Psychical Research, which was founded in 1882. Two of James's friends, F. W. H. Myers and Edmund Gurney, were founder members and William James was a corresponding member from 1884 to 1889, vice-president from 1890 to 1893 and president from 1894 to 1896. James himself never joined the Society, but on one occasion he read to them a paper by William on 'Observations of Certain Phenomena of Trance' and the Preface to *The Turn of the Screw* suggests familiarity with their reports. There James contrasts old-fashioned 'really effective and heart-shaking ghost-stories' with 'the mere modern "psychical" case, washed clean of all queerness as by exposure to a flowing laboratory tap' (*Art of the Novel*, p. 169). The problem is one of 'weak specifications' again: ghosts whose every move is recorded and checked begin to lose their power to frighten. There was another problem too. The apparitions recorded by the Society were on the whole quiet, passive, even benign – far from the atmosphere of brooding evil James hoped to create:

Recorded and attested 'ghosts' are. . . as little expressive, as little dramatic, above all as little continuous and conscious and responsive, as is consistent with their taking the trouble. . . to appear at all. . . I had to decide in fine between having my apparitions correct and having my story 'good' – that is producing my impression of the dreadful, my designed horror.

(*Art of the Novel*, p. 174)

Nevertheless, James's ghosts are much closer to recorded apparitions than to the melodramatic horrors of Gothic tradition. They take a recognisable human shape, appear at any time of the day or night and are invariably silent (the most worrying difference between the tale and the opera), and it has been suggested that James filled out the details of the governess's experiences from cases recorded in the Proceedings of the Society. In one such case, a governess was one evening going up to the room which she shared with one of her pupils:

when just as I reached the top of the stairs I plainly saw the figure of a female dressed in black, with a large white collar or kerchief, very dark hair, and pale face. . . She moved slowly and went into the room, the door of which was open.

A few months later the governess was in the schoolroom when the same figure appeared and 'seemed to go up one step of the stairs'; two of the girls in the governess's charge also claimed to have seen the figure 'while sitting in the schoolroom rather late' and once when returning from a walk, one of them looked through the window 'and saw a lady standing at the bottom of the stairs'. The similarities – the pale-faced figure dressed in black, the appearance in the schoolroom and on the stairs – are minor but they do suggest that James might have been attempting some kind of compromise between current evidence and traditional effects, to give the ghost story new authority by investing up-to-date ghosts with old terrors.[4]

Suggested links between *The Turn of the Screw* and the Psychical Research Society naturally tend to endorse the view that the ghosts, or at least the evil, exist independent of the governess, though they do allow for different explanations of their source. It might be that the governess sees actual ghosts which the children are unable to see: cases of ghosts appearing to isolated members of a gathering are recorded by the Society. Or it might be that the governess's telepathic response to the presence of evil – either in the children or generally at Bly – manifests itself in her visions of the source of that evil, a theory which would again be supported by the Society's Proceedings. Ambiguity about the children's moral condition remains.

Critics doubtful about the governess's reliability have explored contemporary psychological theory for possible sources for James's portrait. Again William James provides a link, as does James's younger sister Alice. Alice James, a fascinating and tragic figure, was an invalid for most of her life and from 1884 until her death in 1892 had lived in England, in Bournemouth, where Henry was a frequent and attentive visitor. She died of cancer, but she suffered throughout her life from neurasthenia which was undoubtedly psychological in origin and which involved occasional 'violent turns of hysteria'. William James was of course professionally as well as personally interested in Alice's case (he published *The Principles of Psychology* in 1890) and in 1891, at his suggestion, hypnotism was tried as a therapy. This followed the theories of the great French specialist Charcot, with whom William had studied, but whose work was in the process of being superseded by Breuer and Freud, whose *Studien über Hysterie* appeared in 1895. James was deeply involved in Alice's treatment and might well have read contemporary psychological theory in an effort to help her. It is impossible to say whether he continued to do so after Alice's death; whether, at William's recommendation, he actually read Freud and found there models for his governess. It has been suggested that one of Freud's cases, that of Miss Lucy R., is strikingly close to *The Turn of the Screw*. An English governess of two children in Vienna came to Freud suffering from depression and lassitude and complaining that the housekeeper, cook and maid in her household, finding her too proud for her position, were intriguing against her and telling stories about her to the children's grandfather. In an intimate interview with their father she was persuaded against resigning her post. Freud encouraged her to admit that she was in love with the father as a result of this interview and having admitted that, her symptoms disappeared. Apart from the instant infatuation with the figure in authority, comparable with James's governess's love for the uncle, there are other details – children taking a letter, jealousy of friends of the family kissing the children, Lucy R.'s fear that her feelings would be discerned – which could have suggested details in James's tale. The evidence is precariously circumstantial, however. What *is* worth noting is that the general problem, described by Freud as 'conversion hysteria', could be seen to explain James's governess's behaviour: having fallen in love with the uncle, the governess is bitterly disappointed to receive only the curtest of notes with the letter dismissing Miles from school and this apparently minor incident, repressed into the subconscious, works itself out through inventions and hallucinations.[5]

And if James did not read Freud, one critic suggests, Alice James herself provides sufficient material to account for the governess. *The Turn of the Screw* might be James's fictional exploration of his sister's case, elaborately disguised of course. Indeed, Archbishop Benson's sons knew nothing of the anecdote recorded in the *Notebooks*. Might James have exaggerated its prominence in a careful attempt to obscure the more personal source. . . ?[6] But we are moving too far towards irresponsible and unhelpful speculation, and too far from *The Turn of the Screw*. James might have read Freud – or his own observations might illustrate and endorse Freud's theories. It is impossible to be any more certain about the relationship between the two.

Sticking to the much more reliable evidence of James's other publications from this period, we can place *The Turn of the Screw* thematically and technically in his development. James recorded the Archbishop's story on 12 January 1895. On 5 January he had

suffered the most painful disappointment in his career when he had
been booed and jeered off the stage at the end of the first night of his
play *Guy Domville*. At the beginning of the 1890s James had
devoted himself, with great hopes, to writing for the theatre. The
reception of *Guy Domville* convinced him that popular success in
that form would always elude him and in his notebook on 23 January he rededicates himself to fiction:

> I take up my *own* old pen again – the pen of all my old unforgettable efforts
> and sacred struggles. . . Large and full and high the future still opens. It is
> now indeed that I may do the work of my life. (p. 179)

His brave words were prophetic. During the later nineties James
embarked on his most experimental period, breaking decisively with
the Victorian tradition of fictional realism in which an on the whole
omniscient narrator tells the reader about characters and events
which seem to be in his or her complete control. For James, 'realism'
meant internalising experience, presenting events from the limited
point of view of one, or sometimes two or three, participants, with
all the attendant doubts about reliability and 'truth'. His later novels
explore and demonstrate the modern sense that we are locked within
our individual consciousnesses with only our own subjective percep-
tions to rely on. As T. S. Eliot put it in *The Waste Land*:

> . . . I have heard the key
> Turn in the door once and turn once only
> We think of the key, each in his prison
> Thinking of the key, each confirms a prison. . .

The Turn of the Screw, with the exception of the opening 'frame',
is told entirely from the governess's point of view. It was immediately
preceded by *What Maisie Knew*, where the various liaisons of
Maisie's divorced parents are seen through the child's eyes; it was followed by the suggestively-titled tale *In the Cage*, in which a telegraph
operator weaves fictions about her various clients based on the
limited view gleaned from the telegrams they send. And from these
shorter experimental works James went on to write the great novels
of his maturity: *The Ambassadors, The Wings of the Dove* and *The
Golden Bowl*.

James's disappointing experience of the theatre was not wasted.
He had struggled to learn to write economically for the stage (he
once lamented that 'within two hours' the dramatist must 'present
and solve the problem he has set himself, or he is doomed')[7] and he
now applied the lesson to his fiction, expressing his epistemological

uncertainties through 'dramatic' techniques. In the Preface to *The Awkward Age*, a novel published in 1899, James talks of his method in terms of 'the successive Acts of a Play' and in the Preface to *What Maisie Knew* he describes this '"scenic" law' in more detail: the subject is explored and presented through a series of 'scenes', representative dramatic encounters as in a play, which alternate with material organised 'by a quite other law' – authorial comment of some kind, or internalised speculation by one of the characters, for example. James describes this other material as 'all preparative' for the 'scenes' themselves: it complements or qualifies our reaction to them, but in these experimental novels the firm direction, impossible for the dramatist, which omniscient authorial commentary gives to our judgements in traditional realist fiction is withheld. *The Awkward Age* consists very largely of dialogue and any authorial comment remains tentative – 'it might have been seen that': in *What Maisie Knew* the 'preparative' passages are concerned with the limited field of what Maisie herself 'might be conceived to have *understood* – to have been able to interpret and appreciate' (*Art of the Novel*, pp. 110, 157–8). The onus of interpretation is on the reader and this lack of authorial direction makes an awareness of the difficulties involved in judging and interpreting characters and their words central to our reading of these novels.

This alternation of 'scene' with an equivocal framing narrative exactly describes the method of *The Turn of the Screw*. We remember the tale as a series of dramatic encounters – the governess's visions of Quint and Miss Jessel, the two scenes with Flora by the lake, the confrontations with Miles – and our reactions, or rather the uncertainty of our reactions, to those encounters is prepared for and reinforced by the intervening passages of explanation and self-analysis which are of course limited to the governess's point of view. For the librettist, James's scenes provide an ideal structure, exploited to the full in Myfanwy Piper's series of short representative encounters, *The Journey, The Welcome, The Letter, The Tower*, etc.; Britten's music has the difficult complementary role of suggesting the insecurity created in James's 'preparative' passages.

Myfanwy Piper has said that what fascinated her in *The Turn of the Screw* was the 'vulnerability of innocence at all ages' and she imported into James a line from W. B. Yeats's poem 'The Second Coming': 'The ceremony of innocence is drowned'.[8] The theme of innocence and experience, of innocence challenged or exploited, recurs throughout James's work. In the earlier part of his career, when he was known as the writer of 'international' tales, James wrote of innocent Americans confronting the complexities of an old and corrupt civilisation in Europe. In *Daisy Miller* (1878), which was a huge popular success, the fresh, brash young American girl is finally destroyed by rigid European *mores*; in *The Portrait of a Lady* (1881), another of James's best-known novels, Isabel Archer's innocent assumptions about her personal freedom are tragically modified when she realises that she has been manipulated by her husband and the sinister Madame Merle. During the nineties James seemed to be particularly concerned with the innocence of children and adolescents, and experience in this context takes on a specifically sexual significance. Maisie in *What Maisie Knew*, passed from hand to hand by her parents and their various partners, is forced into knowledge of their promiscuity and herself learns the art of manipulation, in self-defence and in her affection for Sir Claude, one of her mother's lovers, but she remains miraculously uncorrupted; in *The Awkward Age* the adolescent Nanda Brookenham is similarly thrust into the drawing-room world of adult intrigue and though she too maintains a kind of moral integrity, she loses the man she loves, who expects conventional innocence in the girl he marries; and in *The Turn of the Screw* the relationships between Quint and Miss Jessel and the children, if not themselves sexual, at least involve the children's knowledge of Quint and Miss Jessel's affair, a knowledge explored with unJamesian explicitness in the film *The Nightcomers*.

James's attitude to innocence was far from simple. In one of his most important essays, 'The Art of Fiction', he says that 'the essence of moral energy is to survey the whole field';[9] full moral responsibility is impossible without knowledge. So in *The Portrait of a Lady*, for example, Isabel achieves moral maturity and freedom not at the beginning of the novel when she is so sure that she *is* free, but when she is in full knowledge of her exploited position. In the novels of the nineties James explores the possibility of knowledge remaining free of corruption, so that Nanda's and Maisie's integrity provides, by contrast, a devastating indictment of their elders' selfish and ruthless manoeuvres. Innocence in such a society can be positively dangerous – Nanda's sheltered cousin runs wild when she gains the adult status of marriage. James explores too the difference between knowledge and prurience and in *The Turn of the Screw* we have two kinds of innocence: the children's, which might, like Nanda's and Maisie's, be essentially untainted by their knowledge of Quint and Miss Jessel; and the governess's, the product of a sheltered country upbringing, *innocence* ≠ *ignorance?*

which could make her reactions to Mrs Grose's account of Quint dangerously inappropriate. 'The more I go over it, the more I see in it, and the more I see in it more I fear. I don't know what I *don't* see – what I *don't* fear!'[10] The governess's unbridled imaginings might be justified; they might on the other hand be prompted by her fearful yet fascinated ignorance.

The governess of course never describes in detail exactly what it is she fears. Like James, she avoids 'weak specifications'. Some critics have been less reticent. Was the relationship between Quint and Miles, and perhaps that between Miss Jessel and Flora, actually homosexual? Did the children witness Quint and Miss Jessel's sexual intimacy? Such factual speculations clearly limit James's tale, but they do remind us that it is importantly concerned with the power of sexuality.

power of sexuality

Similar speculations must have crossed the minds of some contemporary reviewers. When *The Turn of the Screw* was published in book form in October 1898, a reviewer in *The Independent* recoiled violently:

'The Turn of the Screw' is the most hopelessly evil story that we have ever read in any literature, ancient or modern. How Mr. James could, or how any man or woman could, choose to make such a study of infernal human debauchery, for it is nothing else, is unaccountable.

The Bookman was less shrill, but flatly denied the possibility of 'the continuity and the extent of the corruption as suggested here'. On the whole, however, the reviews were enthusiastic:

magic of evil

. . . 'The Turn of the Screw', is such a deliberate, powerful, and horribly successful study of the magic of evil . . . as our language has not produced since Stevenson wrote his 'Jekyll and Hyde' tale. . .

It is hardly necessary to say that Mr. James's tale has nothing in common with the ordinary ghost story; it is altogether on a higher plane both of conception and art.

And even the *Independent* reviewer acknowledged that the tale 'exhibits Mr. James's genius in a powerful light'. Almost all these contemporary critics accepted the governess's version of events without question, but an anonymous reviewer in *The Critic* has the distinction of being the first to question her integrity, and to link the tale with *In the Cage*:

The heroine of 'In the Cage' carries her divinations far enough in all conscience, but at least she has real people and tangible telegrams as a basis for her mental processes. The subject-matter of *The Turn of the Screw* is also made up of feminine intuitions, but the heroine. . . has nothing in the least substantial upon which to base her deep and startling cognitions. She perceives what is beyond all perception, and the reader who begins by questioning whether she is supposed to be sane ends by accepting her conclusions and thrilling over the horrors they involve.[11]

In thus singling out the governess's state of mind, this early reviewer hit on the alternative approach to *The Turn of the Screw* – which is to some extent endorsed by the tale's next published appearance. This was in 1908 in the New York Edition of James's works, carefully supervised by James himself, where *The Turn of the Screw* appears not in the volume containing some of James's other ghost stories (*Owen Wingrave, The Friends of the Friends, Sir Edmund Orme,* for example), but in a volume together with *The Aspern Papers* and *The Liar,* two other tales in which we gradually learn to question the narrator's reliability.

The *Critic* reviewer seems to end up believing the governess's narrative, but not before the possibility of a different narrative has been aired. What then, in more detail, *are* these alternatives, these two stories which exist side by side within the one tale?

In the first story, generally accepted for at least twenty years after *The Turn of the Screw* was published, a young girl 'fluttered, anxious' (*The Turn of the Screw,* p. 11) comes up to London from the country to answer an advertisement for a governess. Her employer, the uncle of two orphaned children, is a charming bachelor whom she inevitably finds extremely attractive and who makes the odd stipulation that she shall take sole responsibility for the children, bothering him about them under no circumstances. This is the first challenge to her courage and maturity and she rises to it, accepting the job on these strange terms – not least because the uncle 'put the whole thing to her as a kind of favour, an obligation he should gratefully incur' (p. 11). She goes down to Bly, the uncle's country house in Essex where the children live, and is met by the dependable, 'wholesome' (p. 15) housekeeper, Mrs Grose, and by the little girl, Flora, whose angelic beauty immediately wins her affection. That night she is too excited to sleep much and thinks she hears at one point a child's cry and then, later, footsteps past her door, but she thinks no more about it.

The first worrying occurrence is the arrival of a letter from the little boy Miles's headmaster to say that Miles will not be accepted back at school, but giving no explanation. Mrs Grose refuses to believe that Miles is wicked, apart from the usual pranks boys get up to, and when the governess meets Miles on his arrival from school and finds him as charming as his sister, she agrees and decides to do and say nothing about the letter. During their conversation about Miles, Mrs Grose lets slip that the previous governess, also 'young and pretty' (p. 21), died after leaving Bly, though Mrs Grose was never told what she died of. 'Young and pretty', says Mrs Grose, 'was the way he liked everyone!' (p. 22). She hurriedly claims that 'he' refers to the children's uncle, but her confusion suggests that she had originally referred to someone else.

Several delightful weeks pass as the governess gets to know and love her charges but the idyll is broken when the apparitions begin. The governess sees the figure of a strange man on one of the towers of the house, but does not mention it until she sees the same figure staring in through a window and is suddenly certain that he is looking not for her but for someone else, someone she quickly identifies as the children. From the governess's description, Mrs Grose identifies the figure as Peter Quint, the master's former valet, who to Mrs Grose's disgust had spent a lot of time with Miles – he was 'Too free with everyone!' (p. 40). But Peter Quint is dead, and the governess realises that what faces her is a battle for the possession of Miles – of Miles, and of Flora, for a second apparition, that of Flora's former governess, Miss Jessel, begins to appear and Mrs Grose is forced to admit that there was 'everything' between Quint and Miss Jessel: 'The fellow was a hound' (p. 48). The children never mention Quint and Miss Jessel, in spite of their former closeness, and after further appearances from the ghosts and incidents when the children seem to have plotted to get away to join them, the governess becomes convinced that Miles and Flora are in league with Quint and Miss Jessel, frighteningly corrupt beneath their angelic appearance. These incidents culminate in Flora's escape to the lake to meet Miss Jessel. The governess, but not Mrs Grose, sees Miss Jessel and finally challenges Flora with her name, but Flora remains loyal to her former governess and her 'incomparable childish beauty had suddenly failed, had quite vanished' (p. 101). The conflict makes Flora ill and in her delirium she uses 'really shocking' language which convinces Mrs Grose that the governess's interpretation of the situation is accurate.

Mrs Grose leaves with Flora for London, hoping to save her by removing her from the ghosts' influence, and the governess is left alone with Miles to battle for his soul. In her extremity, she has finally given in and written to the children's uncle but the letter disappeared before it was posted and she now challenges Miles with this theft and with his expulsion from school. He admits to taking the letter, 'To see what you said about me' (p. 117); at school his crime was not theft but, like Flora, he 'said things' (p. 119), passing on to those he liked the language and the experience gained from his closeness to Quint. The governess, elated with the victory of having secured his confession, urges him to tell her in detail what the 'things' were, and at this moment Quint appears. She forces Miles to name Quint, thus exorcising his influence: 'They are in my ears still, his supreme surrender of the name and his tribute to my devotion' (p. 121). But the tragic price of exorcism is Miles's life: 'We were alone with the quiet day, and his little heart, dispossessed, had stopped' (p. 121).

Throughout this story the governess's motives and conduct are impeccable. Faced, virtually alone, with the children's corrupted innocence her love for them and her moral integrity are finally, albeit tragically, triumphant. Her account of events bears out the character reference given at the beginning of the tale by Douglas (the *Prologue* in the opera), who knew her later and who now owns 'the thin old-fashioned gilt-edged album' (p. 14) in which she recorded her experience: 'She was the most agreeable woman I've ever known in her position; she would have been worthy of any whatever' (p. 9). This opening 'frame' can be seen as powerful evidence for the governess's case (and it is interesting that the *Prologue* in the opera is the closest any adaptation comes to reproducing it). It offers independent testimony to her worth and, importantly, focuses on the children's corruption as the 'turn of the screw' which makes the tale particularly horrible and affecting. This, as we have seen, was the emphasis in James's original 'germ' recorded in his notebook and comments by James on other occasions seem again to endorse the governess's integrity. In a letter to H. G. Wells, for example, he talked of the difficulties involved in presenting the governess:

> The grotesque business I had to make her picture and the childish psychology I had to make her trace and present, were, for me at least, a very difficult job, in which absolute lucidity and logic, a singleness of effect, were imperative. Therefore I had to rule out subjective complications of her own – play of tone etc.; and keep her impersonal save for the most obvious and indispensable little note of neatness, firmness and courage – without which she wouldn't have had her data.[12]

He refers to this interchange with Wells in the Preface and again defends himself against Wells's accusation that the governess is not presented fully enough: 'She has "authority", which is a good deal to have given her, and I couldn't have arrived at so much had I clumsily tried for more' (*Art of the Novel*, p. 174). And in a Notebook entry from 1900, when James is planning his long, finally unfinished ghost story *The Sense of the Past*, he describes his ideal as 'something as simple as *The Turn of the Screw*, only different and less grossly and merely apparitional' (*Notebooks*, p. 299).

It is this first story which the opera comes perilously close to endorsing in giving the ghosts singing parts and including, for example, the scene between Miles and Quint (*At Night*) in which their words have no direct source in James's text – though the scene can of course be interpreted as an expression of the imaginative, liberating appeal Quint held for Miles when he was alive ('I am all things strange and bold. . .'), which Miles now misses terribly, restricted as he is by the governess's over-protective affection. The first story is certainly the version offered by William Archibald's play *The Innocents* (1950), in spite of a short introduction claiming that 'the question of whether they were literal ghosts or figments of the mind' is left up to the audience to decide. Archibald simplifies the nuances and understatements of James's story: Mrs Grose offers far more graphic details about the conduct of Quint's and Miss Jessel's relationship; Flora sees Miss Jessel in a scene without the governess present, and holds out her hand to her; and in the last conversation between the governess and Miles, the stage direction describes Miles as 'fully aware of Quint' while the governess is still unaware, and, challenged by the governess, Miles keeps repeating 'He'll hurt me', finally collapsing not in the governess's arms but on the staircase. The evil remains firmly outside the governess.

Apart from its success simply as a ghost story, in which James has certainly achieved his aim of 'causing the situation to reek with the air of Evil' (*Art of the Novel*, p. 175), this first story lends itself to allegorical interpretation and has been seen by many critics as a Faustian drama in which the governess and the ghosts, the Good and Bad Angels, do battle for the children's souls. It becomes a story about the dual nature of man, a little lower than the angels yet prey to the temptation of evil, and some commentators have even gone as far as to identify the uncle with the figure of God, remaining aloof from his creation and leaving humanity free to choose salvation or damnation. The imagery of light and dark, beauty and ugliness, which pervades the tale seems to support this interpretation. When she first meets Flora, the governess is delighted and moved by her 'angelic beauty', her 'beatific. . . radiant image', as of 'one of Raphael's holy infants' (p. 16), but this incomparable beauty later vanishes and Flora becomes 'hideously hard' and 'an old, old woman' in the governess's eyes (pp. 101, 96). Bly is initially a place of 'beauty and dignity' with an Edenic 'charm of stillness' (p. 25), which gives way to autumn with its grey sky and withered garlands, its bared spaces and scattered dead leaves' (p. 73). And another suggestive set of ideas emphasises the governess's embattled position. She talks of 'the extraordinary flight of heroism the occasion demanded of me' (p. 42), of her opportunity to 'absolutely save' the children (p. 39), and in the last chapter the battle is explicitly identified: 'It was like fighting with a demon for a human soul' (p. 117). The story's focus on corrupted *children*, symbols of man's pre-lapsarian innocence, is central to these interpretations. As one critic puts it: 'Miles and Flora become the childhood of the race.' A subtler variation on this allegorical reading is offered by another critic, Dorothea Krook, who takes account of the fact that Miles has to die and of many readers' mistrust of the governess, by arguing that the governess's spiritual triumph is tainted by her sin of pride and her selfish desire for possession. 'I was infatuated – I was blind with victory' (p. 119) says the governess of her last struggle with Miles – and the tale warns us against the catastrophic consequences of such infatuation.[13] In Myfanwy Piper's libretto, the governess's last words, 'What have we done between us?', suggest a similar ambivalence about where responsibility lies. The tragedy is firmly that of the children – as James said in a letter: 'ah, the exposure indeed, the helpless plasticity of childhood that isn't dear or sacred to *some*body!'[14]

In the second story the children are still tragic victims, but victims of the governess's delusions rather than of any supernatural powers. What we have to remember, as the *Critic* reviewer saw, is that we only have the governess's word for anything that happened. The imagery of light and darkness, of spiritual battle, is hers, a way of explaining her experiences to herself. She casts herself in the role of heroine and protectress and we, able to see more clearly than she ever can, have to read between the lines of her narrative to get at the truth.

In this second story, then, the young girl who comes up to London, the sheltered daughter of a country vicar, becomes immediately infatuated with her employer, 'such a figure as had never risen, save in a dream or an old novel' (p. 11) before her. Because of her love she agrees to his terms of employment, eager to impress and attract him by carrying them out to the letter. On her arrival at Bly she is similarly swept away by the grandeur of the place, 'a different affair from my own scant home', with its long mirrors 'in which, for the first

textual differentiation b/w different worlds
→ kids on / years up

time, I could see myself from head to foot' and the appropriately deferential Mrs Grose (p. 15). With a mixture of apprehension and exultation, she finds herself in a position of power for the first time: 'Well, I was, strangely, at the helm!' (p. 18).

Her first problem is the letter from the headmaster dismissing Miles from school. It arrives with a covering note from the uncle who has not even bothered to open it and whose curtness deeply disappoints the governess, so much so that it takes her a long time to get round to opening the second letter. When she does, the news of Miles's expulsion shocks her deeply as something outside her limited, conventional experience, and in spite of the fact that the letter offers no explanation and in the face of Mrs Grose's protestations, she jumps to the conclusion that Miles is 'an injury to the others' (p. 20). It is she who introduces the suggestion that Miles's wickedness, which Mrs Grose sees simply as the healthy rebellion of a small boy, might have the power to 'corrupt' (p. 21). This is the first example of the way in which the governess's over-active imagination compensates for her lack of actual experience; her own innocence is a dangerous limitation, making her incapable of seeing moral problems in proportion. What Miles's expulsion does mean, however, is that she now enjoys sole authority over him, an enjoyment fuelled by her jealous 'passion of tenderness' for him (p. 23), which, it is later suggested, contains more than a hint of sexual attraction.

The pattern of innocence, fantasy and repression set up in the incident of the letter explains the governess's behaviour throughout the tale. Subconsciously she is deeply disturbed by the strength of her frustrated feelings for the uncle and her imagination feeds on Mrs Grose's careless hint about another man who liked them 'young and pretty' to produce her hallucinatory vision of the man on the tower. Only when the vision appears a second time and Mrs Grose finds the governess 'white as a sheet' does she tell the housekeeper about the figure. Mrs Grose, wholesome but superstitious and suggestible, identifies Quint from the least specific details of the governess's description – the fact that the figure wore no hat, that he 'looked like an actor', that he was handsome but 'never – no, never! – a gentleman' (pp. 36–7). The details Mrs Grose later supplies about Quint's relationship with Miss Jessel and their influence over the children give the governess her self-justifying explanations for her experience: her internal battle between her awakened sexual identity and 'the teachings of my small, smothered life' (p. 24) becomes in her imagination a battle for the souls of the adored children. Undoubtedly Miles and Flora learnt things from Quint and Miss Jessel which were not normally part of a Victorian child's education, but the problem is again one of proportion. The governess's capacity for over-interpretation became clear very early. Her interpretations are now inspired by her concern for self-justification, both in Mrs Grose's eyes and, ultimately, in the uncle's, and she sees the most sinister implications in the children's innocent questions and rebellious pranks. There is not a shred of objective evidence to suggest that the children ever see the 'ghosts'.

In the climactic scene with Flora at the lake the governess, with no justification other than her own imaginative conviction, challenges Flora: 'Where, my pet, is Miss Jessel?' (p. 98). Her belief in her own position is so strong that the image of Miss Jessel then appears unmistakably to the governess, but her shriek of 'She's there, she's there!' horrifies Mrs Grose and terrifies Flora, who clings to Mrs Grose for comfort and protection:

'Take me away, take me away – oh, take me away from *her!*'
'From *me*?' I panted.
'From *you* – from you!' she cried.   (p. 101)

Not for the first time, the narrative identifies the governess with the ghosts through an ambiguous pronoun, making the governess herself the predator. The same technique is used in the final scene with Miles. Mrs Grose has taken Flora, who is suffering from a kind of nervous breakdown brought on by her terror of the governess, to London. The bad language Flora used in her delirium convinced Mrs Grose that the governess was right about the ghosts' influence. Of course, it proves no such thing, only the fact that influence existed while Quint and Miss Jessel were alive and that the children, aware of Mrs Grose's disapproval, have since kept their knowledge to themselves. Miles and the governess are left alone. Miles has heard about what happened and is nervous of the governess. Small wonder that when he confesses to having taken her letter, desperate to know why he is being kept from school, and the governess 'with a moan of joy' holds him to her breast, she feels 'in the sudden fever of his little body the tremendous pulse of his little heart' (p. 117). As the governess's questioning becomes more aggressive, Miles's nervousness increases, a nervousness the governess attributes to the presence of Quint. Miles's crime at school was that, like Flora, he 'said things', enough to expel him from a respectable private school, and for a moment the governess feels 'the appalling alarm of his being perhaps innocent' (p. 119). Her inappropriate use of 'alarm' betrays her fatally confused values: self-justification rather than the welfare of the children is her main concern. When the governess starts to shriek 'No more, no more' to Quint Miles can only assume she sees Miss Jessel again. She corrects him, but will not herself name Quint, believing that for Miles to name him is to prove and exorcise the influence. Again, the proof is dubious: it is a very short speculative step for Miles from Miss Jessel to Quint:

'It's not Miss Jessel! But it's at the window – straight before us. It's *there* – the coward horror, there for the last time!'
At this, after a second in which his head made the movement of a baffled dog's on a scent and then gave a frantic little shake for air and light, he was at me in a white rage, bewildered, glaring vainly over the place and missing wholly, though it now, to my sense, filled the room like the taste of poison, the wide, overwhelming presence.
'It's *he?*'
I was so determined to have all my proof that I flashed into ice to challenge him. 'Whom do you mean by "he"?'
'Peter Quint – you devil!' His face gave again, round the room, its convulsed supplication. 'Where?'   (p. 121)

Again the governess is syntactically identified with the devil and as she crushes Miles to her, blinded by her 'victory', she frightens him, literally, to death.

Critics committed to this second story defend themselves, like their adversaries, with evidence from the opening frame and from James's letters and Preface. The introductory frame certainly emphasises the central importance of the haunted children, but it emphasises too the complicating factor of the governess's love for the uncle (or is it for Miles?). And this reflects on Douglas himself who was more than a little in love with his sister's governess when he knew her ten years after the affair at Bly: 'Oh yes, don't grin: I liked her extremely and am glad to this day to think she liked me too' (p. 9), a fact which might well have limited his reading of the governess's experience. James's emphasis in letters on his aim to capture the impression 'of the communication to the children of the most infernal imaginable evil and danger' begs the question – a communication from whom?[15] His comments in the Preface have an ambiguity worthy of the tale itself. I have already quoted his assertion that the governess has 'authority', but just what he means by that is called into question by what he says immediately before:

It was 'déjà très-joli', in 'The Turn of the Screw', please believe, the general proposition of our young woman's keeping crystalline her record of so many intense anomalies and obscurities – *by which I don't of course mean her explanation of them, a different matter.*

(Art of the Novel, p. 173; my italics.)

Earlier in the Preface James describes the tale as 'a piece of ingenuity pure and simple, of cold artistic calculation, an *amusette* to catch those not easily caught' (p. 172). Does he mean to catch those not usually susceptible to ghost stories, or those too quick to read this particular ghost story in the way they would read others? Is the 'turn of the screw' simply the involvement of innocent children, or the dawning realisation that their apparent protector is the real predator?

One of the most famous, but rather simplistic, early versions of the second story was Edmund Wilson's 'Freudian' interpretation.[16] This was Freudian not in the sense that Wilson understood and applied the complexities of Freud's analysis of neurosis, but in its identification of very obvious 'Freudian symbols' – Quint's first appearance on a tower, Miss Jessel's by a lake where Flora is busily engaged in making a boat by pushing one piece of wood into a small hole in another – which Wilson related to the governess's (and later James's) repressed sexuality. Wilson, among others, shifted the tale's focus from the children to the deluded governess and for a time critical argument went backwards and forwards rather at the level of 'No she wasn't' – 'Yes she was', one of the main bones of contention being Mrs Grose's ability to identify Quint from the governess's description. This has been accounted for in various ways. When the figure first appears, the governess says only that she was certain it was not the master. Between the first and second appearances she checks in the village in an attempt to identify the 'intruder', as she admits to Mrs Grose, who asks whether it was someone from the village: 'Nobody – nobody. I didn't tell you, but I made sure' (p. 35). In the village she might easily have heard of Quint and, with her capacity for imaginative embellishment, used him to explain her vision. The problem then, of course, is that she could hardly have failed to hear too of Quint's death, yet when Mrs Grose tells her of it, she 'shrieks' in surprised horror (p. 37). This *can* be explained as, perhaps unconscious, deception on the governess's part. The alternative explanation, which I used in my account of the second story, involves a close reading of the conversation between the governess and Mrs Grose in which the governess, as she does in all their conversations, skilfully plays on Mrs Grose's simplicity and suggestibility, seizing hints and completing Mrs Grose's sentences for her. In this case, she detects

at the beginning in Mrs Grose 'the far-away faint glimmer of a consciousness more acute. . . It comes back to me that I thought instantly
of this as something I could get from her' (p. 35). And Mrs Grose
seizes on the governess's first, least specific detail, 'He has no hat'
(p. 36), and on the suggestion that the figure looked like an actor. The
housekeeper's social and moral hostility to Quint, a resentment still
very much alive, her eagerness to identify him with any kind of threat
to the children, make her an unwitting accomplice for the governess.

The problem of Mrs Grose's identification of Quint is certainly a
crux, but the trouble with this kind of critical focus is that it can lead
away from James's text to the kind of 'weak specifications' he wanted
to avoid. Wilson's simplicity appears thoroughly responsible beside
other critics' suggestions that, for example, Mrs Grose is the mother
of the children and the villain of the piece, or that Douglas is in fact
the grown-up Miles, who miraculously did not die! But the responsible alternative reading can never again be ignored, in spite of the
extravagant interpretations it has sometimes been called upon to
sanction. Indeed, to deny the second story when the possibility of
reading *The Turn of the Screw* in that way has been so amply demonstrated, is to reduce James's tale to a very poor thing, unconsciously
confused rather than responsibly ambiguous.

But is a compromise between the two readings possible? Attempts
to account for the governess's experience, even those acknowledging
the alternative, are always unsatisfactory. By explaining and clarify-
ing they cannot hope to do justice to the constant and irreconcilable
ambiguity of James's text. Just a few examples will be enough to suggest its richness and its resistance to successful adaptation. We have
already seen how, in the climactic scene by the lake, Flora's fear
identifies the governess with Miss Jessel. This identification is a frequent technique, sometimes explicit, as in the scene in which the
governess tells Mrs Grose about the first encounter with Miss Jessel,
who 'fixed' Flora with her gaze:

Mrs Grose tried to see it. 'Fixed her?'
'Ah, with such awful eyes!'
She stared at mine as if they might really have resembled them.   (p. 47)

Sometimes the identification is more suggestively made, as earlier in
the same scene:

'She just appeared and stood there – but not so near.'
'And without coming nearer?'
'Oh, for the effect and the feeling, she might have been as close as you!'
My friend, with an odd impulse, fell back a step.   (p. 46)

We have already seen, too, the governess's tendency to embroider and over-interpret events, a tendency reflected in the language of her narrative, where supposition quickly becomes fact. In the night scene in which the governess looks out of the window to see Miles on the lawn below her, she says that he was:

> looking. . . not so much straight at me as at something that was *apparently* above me. There was *clearly* another person above me – there was a person on the tower. . .   (p. 64; my italics)

The change from 'apparently' to 'clearly' might well reflect the governess's growing psychic certainty; it might on the other hand warn us against a certainty based on so little evidence. James revised *The Turn of the Screw* for the New York Edition and most of his revisions increase the ambiguity, replacing verbs of thought by verbs of less certain intuition, for example. One very striking revision occurs at the end of the tale. The governess is defending Miles against Quint:

> 'No more, no more, no more!' I shrieked, as I tried to press him against me, to my visitant.   (p. 120)

This is the 1898 version. In the New York Edition, the sentence reads:

> 'No more, no more, no more!' I shrieked to my visitant as I tried to press him against me.[17]

It is possible to explain the revision away simply in terms of syntactical elegance but James, the master of syntax, can hardly have failed to notice that the change makes the referent of 'him' problematic, drawing attention to the governess's equally problematic relationship with the ghosts.

Pervasive textual ambiguities of this kind cannot be 'solved'. So the answer is not compromise, but a sophisticated reading which keeps both stories in play at once, without the felt need to decide between them. We can actually never be sure what happened at Bly: no interpretation accounts for all the possibilities. The focus shifts, therefore, to the problem of interpretation itself, the governess's – and ours. The governess tries to explain her experience by casting herself as a spiritual saviour or as Jane Eyre: 'Was there a "secret" at Bly – a mystery of Udolpho or an insane, an unmentionable relative kept in unsuspected confinement?' (p. 28); we try to explain the story by assuming it is a ghost story or a psychological study of neurosis. The events and the tale escape our imposed interpretations, and our restricted points of view, our presuppositions, undermine the possibility of 'truth' or certainty. I have already discussed James's experimental exploration of the limited point of view. In *The Turn of the Screw* he uses the technique to revolutionise the traditional popular form of the ghost story and to draw attention to the complex process involved in interpreting what we read. 'What happens?' is no longer a simple question, and this self-consciousness identifies James as one of the earliest exemplars of modernism.

To emphasise this self-conscious aspect of *The Turn of the Screw* is not in any sense to deny its moral importance or 'the air of Evil' which James sought to convey. On the contrary: if all the tale's possible meanings are kept in play at once the effect is enriching rather than reductive. It asks us to think about the possibility and possible effects of the supernatural, about the human capacity for self-delusion, about the power of sexuality, about the equivocal innocence of children – and it can still frighten us. A new dimension is added to the exploration of our capacity for evil. James's tale both celebrates and warns against the power of the imagination: celebrates, because without the governess's imaginative struggle to make sense of her experience and our imaginative commitment to the tale itself, it would fail entirely; warns against, because it demonstrates through its ambiguity and understatement our terrifying ability to supply evil, imaginatively to *create* it. As James said in the Preface, 'Make the reader *think* the evil, make him think it for himself' (*Art of the Novel*, p. 176). Any adaptation has to contend with this difficulty, and this richness, and it is a challenge faced in Britten's music.

The air of the evil
– Why is evil evil!?

2 Myfanwy Piper's 'The Turn of the Screw': libretto and synopsis

PATRICIA HOWARD

To transfer to the operatic stage a story so meticulously constructed to manipulate the responses of a reader poses enormous problems. The chief of these is to retain all the ambiguities of the plot so that the opera-goer, as much as the reader, can 'keep both stories in play at once' (see above, p. 21). Not to attempt this, to settle for either of the simple interpretations of the story, would have been an act of vandalism by no means unparalleled in the history of opera, but totally uncharacteristic of Britten. Myfanwy Piper is clear about the composer's aims: 'Neither Britten nor I ever intended to interpret the work, only to recreate it for a different medium' (Piper in Herbert (ed.), p. 11).

This intention has been questioned. Lord Harewood has suggested that the reading which Vivien Jones identified as the 'first story' – the innocent governess and the objective reality of the ghosts – had priority with Britten: 'Harewood was adamant on the ambivalence of the governess's position. To him it was crucial never to know if she was mad or if everyone else was under the control of a malign influence. Britten felt he had to take sides, and he had decided there was something malign at Bly' (Blyth, p. 82). Mrs Piper, however, offers this insight into Britten's attitude to the story: 'I don't think Ben really took sides: but James's story certainly underlines his own emotional attitude to the corruptibility of innocence. That evil exists whether in life or in the mind. . . and is capable of corrupting – or perhaps not necessarily corrupting but causing the loss of innocence – he was, I think, quite certain. The Governess's good intentions were destroyed by her experiences, whether real or imagined, and her love of Miles was corrupted, in that it became possessiveness and she was aware of it. Hence the last words "What have we done between us?"'[1]

Many productions of the opera endorse only the 'first story' interpretation. To produce the opera so that it favours the 'second story' – the evil emanating wholly from the deluded governess – has

23

also been attempted, though such a production is difficult to bring off unless some of the opera's stage directions are ignored. The libretto, however, is written in such a way that many of the story's ambiguities are retained, and this chapter sets out to show that if any performance of the work offers a single interpretation, it is the producer who has chosen from options left open by the composer and librettist.

The most immediate differences between James's story and Mrs Piper's libretto are structural. The story opens with the house-party, and every detail leading up to the main narration – the locked drawer, the posting of the key, the exactly calculated passage of time before the manuscript can be delivered – serves to 'authenticate' the ghost story itself. This pretended realism is carried forward into the narration of events at Bly. It is 'read' from the governess's own account: a technique which enables her feelings and impressions, her partial knowledge and gradual understanding, or misunderstanding, to play as large a part as the incidents themselves. (Indeed, in the second reading of the story, these feelings and impressions are the only significant incidents.) This narrative technique is essentially literary, and there is no obvious way in which it could be transferred to the opera. The governess is not always on stage and it is the moments when she is absent – notably the scene between the children and the ghosts which concludes Act I and the 'colloquy' between the ghosts which opens Act II – which can seem to stamp as indisputably objective the 'something malign at Bly'.[2]

Practical considerations initially precluded staging the house-party. In post-war Britain the economic vulnerability endemic to opera was at a particularly critical stage, and Britten's chamber operas, which include *The Rape of Lucretia* (1946), *Albert Herring* (1947) and *The Little Sweep* (1949) besides *The Turn of the Screw*, were devised for a small body of both singers and instrumentalists for commercial as well as for artistic reasons.[3] *The Screw* fulfilled the needs of the English Opera Group admirably, requiring only four or five adult singers. But these proved to be too few to recreate the changing moods of James's Christmas party, in which the author begins with a largish gathering of guests which is deliberately depleted of the insensitive and the idly curious to obtain the sympathetic audience of intimates the story requires. Mrs Piper reveals that the possibility of a house-party scene was also rejected on stylistic grounds: a late redrafting which opened the work with a 'rather gay scene from Henry James's introductory ghost story party' was *house party*)

turned down by Britten because it was 'wrong for the tightness of the recreated work' (Piper in Herbert (ed.), p. 11).[4]

The decision to open the opera not with a crowded stage of anonymous guests but with the solitary figure of the narrator yielded an interesting dramatic bonus. In James's story the house-party functions primarily as an introduction, but a sensitive reader can carry forward an awareness of its presence, remembering that the story is being related to this particular audience and it is these assembled guests who will ultimately decide between the two interpretations. In the opera the house-party is 'played' by the audience in the opera house. In Mrs Piper's *Prologue* James's storyteller, Douglas, addresses them directly, and they are more closely involved in judging the evidence of the sixteen incidents the opera sets forth than they could be if another audience were interposed between the narrator and themselves.

It is, then, surprising to discover that the *Prologue* was a comparatively late addition. The opera was to begin with the governess's journey to Bly. After the first few scenes of Act I had already been written and set, however, the producer, Basil Coleman, pointed out that the work risked being 'much too short' (Piper in Herbert (ed.), p. 11). The length of an opera can be crucial to its commercial viability,[5] and it was primarily in response to Coleman's observation that the *Prologue*, which now seems an inevitable introduction to the opera, came to be written (see Chapter 3, p. 65).

The *Prologue* is set in recitative and the libretto follows closely the plain, quasi-realistic diction of James's narrator. Throughout the opera we notice Mrs Piper using phrases and whole conversations from James, though she often elects to sacrifice some of his rhythms, in particular the sequences of unfinished sentences which help to create the atmosphere of *unspoken* imaginings in the tale. Mrs Piper's libretto is a simplification and a condensation of James, as these parallel passages show:

'Then your manuscript – ?'
'Is in old, faded ink, and in the most beautiful hand.'
He hung fire again. 'A woman's. She has been dead these twenty years. She sent me the pages in question before she died.'   (James, p. 8)

It is a curious story.
I have it written in faded ink – a woman's hand, governess to two children – long ago.   (Piper, *Prologue*)[6]

The *Prologue* makes one other point, and makes it so delicately and indeed so elliptically that it would be easy to overlook it. James's introductory scenes make clear the fact that his ghost story is also a love story. The governess falls instantly in love with the guardian and accepts the rather forbidding assignment solely on account of this infatuation:

'She was young, untried, nervous: it was a vision of serious duties and little company, of really great loneliness. She hesitated – took a couple of days to consult and consider. But the salary offered much exceeded her modest measure, and on a second interview she faced the music, she engaged.' And Douglas, with this, made a pause that, for the benefit of the company, moved me to throw in –
'The moral of which was of course the seduction exercised by the splendid young man. She succumbed to it.'
He got up and, as he had done the night before, went to the fire, gave a stir to a log with his foot, then stood a moment with his back to us. 'She saw him only twice.'
'Yes, but that's just the beauty of her passion.'
A little to my surprise, on this, Douglas turned round to me. 'It *was* the beauty of it. There were others,' he went on, 'who hadn't succumbed. He told her frankly all his difficulty – that for several applicants the conditions had been prohibitive. They were, somehow, simply afraid. It sounded dull – it sounded strange; and all the more so because of his main condition.'
'Which was – ?'
'That she should never trouble him – but never, never: neither appeal nor complain nor write about anything; only meet all questions herself, receive all moneys from his solicitor, take the whole thing over and let him alone. She promised to do this, and she mentioned to me that when, for a moment, disburdened, delighted, he held her hand, thanking her for the sacrifice, she already felt rewarded.'   (pp. 13–14)

In the opera the governess's passion is revealed more explicitly in the melodic line than in the deliberately plain phrases of the libretto. But at the conclusion of the scene, Mrs Piper produces a telling verbal counterpart of the handclasp in the story:

She was full of doubts.

But she was carried away: that he, so gallant and handsome,
so deep in the busy world, should need her help.

At last
'I will,' she said.   (*Prologue*; my italics)

And with a richness of means only possible in opera, this declaration with its symbolic marriage vow sets the drama in motion. As the governess sings 'I will', the theme of the opera (musically speaking the opera can be regarded as a theme and variations on the grandest scale – see Chapter 3) is introduced, secretly, almost unnoticed at first, but growing in volume and rising in pitch till it explodes in the nervous, questioning music of the journey to Bly.

For the opera proper Britten and Piper devised a formal scheme which translates the structure of the story into musical conventions:

> When quite early in our discussions the idea of three acts was abandoned and Britten planned the opera in terms of short scenes linked by orchestral passages, the nature of these scenes, except for the first scene of Act II, was clearly dictated by an analysis of the text; what had to be invented were the details.   (Piper in Herbert (ed.), p. 9)

James's structure is crucial to his purpose (see Chapter 1, p. 8). The story is written as a series of episodes because it is concerned with presenting testimony: a chain of separate incidents, we might almost say 'sightings', is offered as the evidence on which the governess bases her conclusions – and on which the house-party guests base theirs. James contrived that the structure should be suggested by the governess herself: 'I remember the whole beginning as a succession of flights and drops, a little see-saw of the right throbs and the wrong' (p. 14). Peter Evans has pointed out that it was essential for the opera to retain this episodic structure: 'Any attempt to construct one continuously unfolding dramatic action would have introduced a causality quite at odds with James's intentions' (Evans, *The Music of Benjamin Britten*, p. 205). The incidents which make up the story are evidence, as much for the audience as for the governess, and by offering them as discrete episodes (only Act II scenes 2–3, Act II scenes 4–5 and Act II scenes 6–7 imply a continuous time-sequence) Britten and Piper retained the judicial presentation of the story.

The opera extracts sixteen scenes from the twenty-four chapters of the story. Two 'sightings' in the story are omitted in the opera, and three scenes in the opera have no explicit basis in James. The scenes are separated from one another by short instrumental interludes which have the double function of presenting variations of great technical ingenuity on the theme of the opera, and also of preparing for the following scenes with evocations of atmosphere or actual scene-painting. The interludes flow from one scene to the next, often overlapping and merging at either end, so that, in spite of the episodic structure of the drama, each act of the opera is a continuous stream of music.

However although the interludes help to give a distinct character to each separate episode of the drama, they cannot convey with any precision the passage of time which plays so important a part in the story:

I waited and waited, and the days, as they elapsed, took something from my consternation. A very few of them, in fact, passing, in constant sight of my pupils, without a fresh incident, sufficed to give to grievous fancies and even to odious memories a kind of brush of the sponge.   (p. 55)

'Losing the sense of time' had been Mrs Piper's criticism of the stage play version of James's story, *The Innocents* by William Archibald (see Chapter 1, p. 14), in which

with great ingenuity, the story was shaped and tidied into a semblance of what the three unities demand, with the idea, no doubt, of concentrating the diffuseness and so increasing, for the stage, the tension and horror. But in losing the sense of time, the shifting of places, the gaps in the action, the long months when nothing and everything happened, by laying it on thick *and* fast, it lost the ambivalence and the drama as well. (Piper in Gishford (ed.), p. 79)

The libretto is certainly much more faithful to James than is *The Innocents*. But the variation–interludes are too short to imply 'the long months when nothing and everything happened' (for example the whole of James's Chapter 13). By presenting the 'drops' without the 'flights' the emphasis of James's story is inevitably altered. The relationship of the libretto to the story can be shown in this chart, though it is necessary to remember that the libretto is based so closely on the actual words of Henry James that phrases, sentences and even short dialogues are sometimes 'borrowed' from one scene to appear in another.

Libretto		Principal sources in James
Prologue		Introduction, pp. 8–14
Act I		
Scene 1	*The Journey*	Chapter 1, p. 14
Scene 2	*The Welcome*	Chapter 1, p. 15
Scene 3	*The Letter*	Chapter 2, pp. 19–24
Scene 4	*The Tower*	Chapter 3, pp. 25–8
Scene 5	*The Window*	Chapters 4–6, pp. 32–9
Scene 6	*The Lesson*	[Chapter 9, pp. 56–7][7]
Scene 7	*The Lake*	Chapters 6–7, pp. 43–9
Scene 8	*At Night*	Chapters 10–11, pp. 62–4, 67–8
Act II		
Scene 1	*Colloquy and Soliloquy*	no source
Scene 2	*The Bells*	Chapters 14–15, pp. 77–82; also Chapter 12, pp. 69–71
Scene 3	*Miss Jessel*	Chapter 15, p. 83
Scene 4	*The Bedroom*	Chapter 17, pp. 87–91
Scene 5	*Quint*	no source
Scene 6	*The Piano*	Chapter 18, pp. 92–4
Scene 7	*Flora*	Chapters 19–20, pp. 98–101
Scene 8	*Miles*	Chapter 21–4, pp. 103–21

The first scenes are built on very slender hints in the story. *The Journey*, originally planned to be the opening of the opera, introduces the governess, full of questions, hopes and apprehensions:

Nearly there.
Very soon I shall know, I shall know, I shall know what's in store for me.

(I. 1)

Her unprompted anticipation of some undefined trouble seems particularly significant for the second reading of the story:

If things go wrong, what shall I do? Who can I ask, with none of my kind to talk to?. . .
Whatever happens, it is I, I must decide.   (my italics)

The phrase 'my kind' recurs in the opera. In the next scene Mrs Grose declares that Flora and Miles 'need their own kind', meaning the governess, whom she sees as compatible with the children on the grounds of both her youth and her intelligence. ('They're far too clever for me! They'll do better now, they'll do better with a young thing.') And Miles, in Act II scene 2, wants to know when he is going back to school – 'I'm growing up, you know. I want my own kind.' What constitutes Miles's 'own kind' is precisely the matter at issue. The governess's imagination supplies the answer: schoolfellows to corrupt as she suspects he corrupted those at his old school. Or perhaps Quint. The recurrent phrase emphasises the isolation of all the characters in the story. The governess and Mrs Grose are divided by class, education and age; the children are kept apart both from their only living relative and from their contemporaries; the ghosts, besides being set apart by their supernatural nature, are carefully distanced, always appearing behind some sort of barrier – the height of a tower, the span of a lake, the thickness of glass. And both express an obsessive desire for companionship:

Quint: I seek a friend –   Isolation
             Obedient to follow where I lead,
             Slick as a juggler's mate to catch my thought . . .
Miss Jessel: I too must have a soul to share my woe . . .   (II. 1)

In James's story we are aware of a subdued bustle of underservants peopling the corridors and grounds at Bly. The opera, of course, has no such presence, and gains in intensity and focus from the more complete isolation of each character.

The Welcome is a substantial scene, drawn from a few sentences in the story:

I remember the whole beginning as a succession of flights and drops, a little see-saw of the right throbs and the wrong. After rising, in town, to meet his appeal, I had at all events a couple of very bad days – found myself doubtful again, felt indeed sure I had made a mistake. In this state of mind I spent the long hours of bumping, swinging coach that carried me to the stopping-place at which I was to be met by a vehicle from the house. This convenience, I was told, had been ordered, and I found, towards the close of the June afternoon, a commodious fly in waiting for me. Driving at that hour, on a lovely day, through a country to which the summer sweetness seemed to offer me a friendly welcome, my fortitude mounted afresh and, as we turned into the avenue, encountered a reprieve that was probably but a proof of the point to which it had sunk. I suppose I had expected, or had dreaded, something so melancholy that what greeted me was a good surprise. I remember as a most pleasant impression the broad, clear front, its open windows and fresh curtains and the pair of maids looking out: I remember the lawn and the bright flowers and the crunch of my wheels on the gravel and the clustered tree-tops over which the rooks circled and cawed in the golden sky. The scene had a greatness that made it a different affair from my own scant home, and there immediately appeared at the door, with a little girl in her hand, a civil person who dropped me as decent a curtsey as if I had been the mistress or a distinguished visitor.   (pp. 14–15)

The libretto changes the events here by introducing both children at once. And it picks up the brief reference to Flora's curtsey to build an elaborate welcome ceremony, the children practising their bows and curtseys to a shimmer of harp figures. Britten's operas are full of ceremonies of greeting or farewell. (*The Little Sweep* has a memorable 'good morning' number and both *Peter Grimes* and *The Rape of Lucretia* make set-piece ensembles out of the act of bidding good night.) The mood here is reassuring. The children are presented as attractively normal, as they pester the wholesome Mrs Grose with questions about their new governess. And the complete absence of foreboding is sustained through the governess's arrival:

How charming they are, how beautiful too. The house and park are so splendid, far grander than I am used to. . . Bly, I begin to love you.   (I. 2)

In the story, James gives even this happy scene an ominous shadow:

It was thrown in as well, from the first moment, that I should get on with Mrs Grose in a relation over which, on my way, in the coach, I fear I had rather brooded. The only thing indeed that in this early outlook might have made me shrink again was the clear circumstance of her being so glad to see me. I perceived within half an hour that she was so glad – stout, simple, plain, clean, wholesome woman – as to be positively on her guard against showing it too much. I wondered even then a little why she should wish not to show it and that, with reflection, with suspicion, might of course have made me uneasy.   (p. 15)

But in the opera the governess's blossoming legato phrases, a welcome lyricism after the spare recitative *Prologue* and the agitated motion of *The Journey*, express nothing but confidence and hope.

James delays Miles's arrival till after the receipt of the letter informing the governess that the boy has been expelled from his school. This sequence of events ensures that when the governess sees Miles for the first time there is already a question in her mind: 'Is he really bad?' (p. 20). Britten and Piper sacrificed this small area of doubt (which is significant for the 'second story' interpretation) for the musical advantages of a set-piece welcome, involving all the 'human' characters, at ease with each other for the first and last time in the opera, in a satisfying ensemble.

The Letter arrives when, in the opera, the governess has already formed an impression of Miles's charm and innocent goodness. As she breaks the news to Mrs Grose that Miles is 'dismissed his school', the children are seen through a window singing and acting the traditional nursery rhyme 'Lavender's blue'. Witnessing this gentle scene, the women conclude that 'the child is an angel' and the school's implied accusation 'a wicked lie' (I. 3).

Later in the opera the window becomes a focal point of the mystery at Bly. Quint makes his second appearance looking through it (in Act I scene 5) and it has, moreover, become customary to stage the last scene of the opera in the schoolroom so that Quint's final appearance is (as it is in James) at the same window.[8] This provides – except for those who are seeing the opera for the first time – a visual clue to the possibility of deception in the children's gentle game, seen as it is through what is to become Quint's window. There is an aural clue, too: the brief entry of the celesta, the special tone colour associated with Quint throughout the opera, mocks Mrs Grose's statement, 'We were far too long alone'. (Were we – are we even now – alone?) Again, this clue is not available to a first-time audience. The celesta has an innately chilling tone colour, but at this stage in the opera the audience has no reason to associate it specifically with the supernatural.

To a first-time audience *The Letter* is a reassuring scene. The governess and Mrs Grose, united in an embrace, dismiss the charge against Miles – the charge which is, incidentally, a serious stumbling block to the second reading of the story. It is the only objective evidence of 'evil' in Miles which takes place before we begin to see events through the governess's eyes. Perhaps, though, James did not intend us to regard a headmaster's judgement as any less fallible than the governess's.

1 English National Opera, 1984, Act I scene 2. Rosanne Brackenridge, Jill Gomez, Nicholas Sillitoe, Margaret Kingsley. Producer, Jonathan Miller; designers, Patrick Robertson and Rosemary Vercoe.

2 Bayerische Staatsoper/Oper der Stadt Köln joint production 1983, Act I scene 5. Isobel Buchanan, Machiko Obata, Allan Bergius, Mechtild Gessendorf. Producer, Michael Hampe; designer, John Gunter.

The Tower is introduced in the opera, as it is in James, with an evocation of 'sweet summer':

> In the first weeks the days were long; they often, at their finest, gave me what I used to call my own hour, the hour when, for my pupils, tea-time and bedtime having come and gone, I had, before my final retirement, a small interval alone. Much as I liked my companions, this hour was the thing in the day I liked most; and I liked it best of all when, as the light faded – or rather, I should say, the day lingered and the last calls of the last birds sounded, in a flushed sky, from the old trees – I could take a turn into the grounds and enjoy, almost with a sense of property that amused and flattered me, the beauty and dignity of the place.
> (p. 25)

If *The Letter* asserted the *children's* innocence, this scene offers evidence of the *governess's* tender vulnerability. Her infatuation with the children's guardian leads her to see her performance of all her duties as an expression of her love for him:

> Only one thing I wish, that I could see him –
> and that he could see how well I do his bidding.
> (I.4)

> One of the thoughts that, as I don't in the least shrink now from noting, used to be with me in these wanderings was that it would be as charming as a charming story suddenly to meet someone. Someone would appear there at the turn of a path and would stand before me and smile and approve. I didn't ask more than that – I only asked that he should *know*; and the only way to be sure he knew would be to see it, and the kind light of it, in his handsome face.
> (p. 26)

Musing on the guardian, half-expecting at any moment to see him, and protesting in words heavy with irony that she is 'alone, tranquil, serene' (I. 4), she becomes aware of a figure on the tower. (The celesta again – compare Act I scene 3 – highlights the word 'alone', and from this point in the opera it is identified with the appearances of Quint.)

James elaborates on the appearance with a tone of curiously clinical self-examination:

> It produced in me, this figure, in the clear twilight, I remember, two distinct gasps of emotion, which were, sharply, the shock of my first and that of my second surprise. My second was a violent perception of the mistake of my first: the man who met my eyes was not the person I had precipitately supposed. There came to me thus a bewilderment of vision of which, after these years, there is no living view that I can hope to give. An unknown man in a lonely place is a permitted object of fear to a young woman privately bred; and the figure that faced me was – a few more seconds assured me – as little anyone else I knew as it was the image that had been in my mind. I had not seen it in Harley Street – I had not seen it anywhere. The place, moreover, in the strangest way in the world, had, on the instant, and by the very fact of its appearance, become a solitude. To me at least, making my statement here with a deliberation with which I have never made it, the whole feeling of the moment returns. It was as if, while I took in – what I did take in – all the rest of the scene had been stricken with death. I can hear again, as I write, the

intense hush in which the sounds of evening dropped. The rooks stopped cawing in the golden sky and the friendly hour lost, for the minute, all its voice. But there was no other change in nature, unless indeed it were a change that I saw with a stranger sharpness. The gold was still in the sky, the clearness in the air, and the man who looked at me over the battlements was as definite as a picture in a frame. That's how I thought, with extraordinary quickness, of each person that he might have been and that he was not. We were confronted across our distance quite long enough for me to ask myself with intensity who then he was and to feel, as an effect of my inability to say, a wonder that in a few instants more became intense.

The great question, or one of these, is, afterwards, I know, with regard to certain matters, the question of how long they have lasted. Well, this matter of mine, think what you will of it, lasted while I caught at a dozen possibilities, none of which made a difference for the better, that I could see, in there having been in the house – and for how long, above all? – a person of whom I was in ignorance. It lasted while I just bridled a little with the sense that my office demanded that there should be no such ignorance and no such person. It lasted while this visitant, at all events – and there was a touch of the strange freedom, as I remember, in the sign of familiarity of his wearing no hat – seemed to fix me, from his position, with just the question, just the scrutiny through the fading light, that his own presence provoked. We were too far apart to call to each other, but there was a moment at which, at shorter range, some challenge between us, breaking the hush, would have been the right result of our straight mutual stare. He was in one of the angles, the one away from the house, very erect, as it struck me, and with both hands on the ledge. So I saw him as I see the letters I form on this page; then, exactly, after a minute, as if to add to the spectacle, he slowly changed his place – passed, looking at me hard all the while, to the opposite corner of the platform. Yes, I had the sharpest sense that during this transit he never took his eyes from me, and I can see at this moment the way his hand, as he went, passed from one of the crenelations to the next. He stopped at the other corner, but less long, and even as he turned away still markedly fixed me. He turned away; that was all I knew. (pp. 26–8)

Some of the phrases used by James are so like a medical case-history that J. Purdon Martin has identified the passage as an accurate description of a known neurological disorder – powerful evidence for the 'second story':

'Turns' or small fits, such as the governess describes, were first recognised in this country by the famous British neurologist, Hughlings Jackson. The feature of those attacks about which he wrote most was what he called the 'dreamy state', a condition of brief duration in which the subject has a visual hallucination – a vision, a dream, very often a reminiscence (he thinks) of something he has seen before or of circumstances he has been in before, which, in many instances, is very vivid. Moreover, while he is 'held' by the vision the patient is not fully conscious of his environment and the defect of awareness may take different forms, according to circumstances. The turns are accompanied by an emotional state – usually shock, anxiety, fear, dread, horror – though Jackson noted that the emotion may sometimes be pleasant. Dostoevsky wrote of his aura: 'a terrible thing is the frightful clearness with which it manifests itself and the rapture with which it fills you'. The patient usually goes pale – observers may say 'deathly pale', 'livid' – and afterwards may flush. When the vision passes off it may be some time before consciousness is fully restored, and, in particular, the patient, though he may behave normally, may not remember what takes place during this period – he has a 'time-gap'.

All these features are described in detail by the governess. Not only did she 'see' the figure on the tower and experience the shock, but, at the same time (she felt) 'the place. . . had become a solitude. . . all the rest of the scene had been stricken with death. . . the intense hush in which the sounds of evening dropped. The rooks stopped cawing in the golden sky and the friendly hour lost for the unspeakable minute all its voice'. The vision was very vivid – 'as definite as a picture in a frame', and afterwards she had a 'time-gap'; 'I cannot say how long in a confusion of curiosity and dread I remained where I had had my collision; I only recall that when I re-entered the house, darkness had quite closed in'.[9]

The opera is forced to condense events and so to ignore the evidence of the time-gap. But it offers strong dramatic compensations. We can, after all, see the figure on the tower, who can be made to look as much like the guardian or a ghoul as the producer chooses. Anthony Besch's production for Scottish Opera (1970; see Chapter 4) drew a strong connecting thread between Quint and the guardian. During the singing of the *Prologue* he had the encounter between the governess and the guardian mimed so that the audience saw 'the governess being engaged by a figure with red curly hair and the foxy features later associated with Peter Quint' (John Higgins, *The Times*, 3 April 1970, p. 12). There is, though, no justification in James for this. The governess's mistaken identification of the figure on the tower in Act I scene 4 is momentary, and caused by her intense longing to see her employer rather than any physical similarity between the guardian and Quint.

As Quint appears, the music urgently quickens the pulse as it moves into an agitated tempo, reiterating a questioning figure which is later given a precise verbal meaning when the governess sings 'Who is it?' (I. 4). Words and music are full of obsessive questions:

Who is it? Who?
Who can it be?
Some servant – no! I know them all.
Who is it, who?
Who can it be?
Some curious stranger? But how did he get in?
Who is it, who?
Some fearful madman locked away there?

Adventurer? Intruder?
Who is it, who?
Who can it be?   (I. 4)

In the story there is quite an interval of time – 'many days' (p. 29)
– before the governess's questions are answered. And the sinister
appearance on the tower is juxtaposed with a reminder of the children's disarming behaviour: 'Both the children had a gentleness. . .
that kept them – how shall I express it? – almost impersonal and certainly quite unpunishable' (p. 31). In the libretto, this reminder is
faithfully retained when scene 5, *The Window*, opens with a second
nursery game. The orchestral writing, however, allows the governess's questions to echo throughout the scene. In Variation IV, which
precedes the scene, the 'Who is it?' motif is transformed into the
brisk accompaniment to the children's song, 'Tom, Tom the Piper's
son', creating an unambiguous pointer to the 'second story', which
would have us believe that the governess now sees the children
through vision which has been tainted or at least distorted by her
experiences before the tower. There is, however, just sufficient
ambivalence in the nursery game, an excess of energy bordering on
violence as the stealing, catching and beating are acted out, for a
producer aiming to advance the 'first story' interpretation to raise
questions in the audience's minds about the children's innocence.
For example, Tom Sutcliffe writes of Jonathan Miller's production at
the Coliseum:

Never have Britten's children less deserved to be called The Innocents. When
Miles asks, 'Now *chase* me,' it's a sexual invitation. Likewise 'Tom was *beat*.'
Dr Miller finds it's a Bergmanesque psycho-drama about incest rather than
paedophilia, though there may have been some of that too.
                                              (*Guardian*, 8 November 1979, p. 11)

Like Act I scene 8 and Act II scene 1, this is a scene which takes place
with the governess off-stage, and thus becomes an invitation to the
producer to 'take sides' in the interpretative conundrum.

As the children career out of the hall, the governess enters in
search of a pair of gloves. She glances at the window and sees Quint
peering into the room. James tells us at once that 'the person looking
straight in was the person who had already appeared' on the tower
(p. 32). Britten conveys the same information by quoting the 'Who is
it?' motif on the celesta – a device which both renews the question
and answers it. There is an even more disturbing sequel to this incident. As Quint disappears, the governess runs outside and takes his
place at the window, looking in:

It was confusedly present to me that I ought to place myself where he had stood. I did so; I applied my face to the pane and looked, as he had looked, into the room. As if, at this moment, to show me exactly what his range had been, Mrs Grose, as I had done for himself just before, came in from the hall. With this I had the full image of a repetition of what had already occurred. She saw me as I had seen my own visitant; she pulled up short as I had done; I gave her something of the shock that I had received. She turned white, and this made me ask myself if I had blanched as much. She stared, in short, and retreated on just *my* lines, and I knew she had then passed out and come round to me and that I should presently meet her. I remained where I was, and while I waited I thought of more things than one. But there's only one I take space to mention. I wondered why *she* should be scared.   (p. 33)

The confusion of identity implied by this sequence of actions is highly suggestive. The governess is momentarily compelled *to take Quint's place* and finds that she has the same effect on Mrs Grose as Quint had on her – evidence not to be ignored that it is the governess not the children who is the catalyst in the tragedy at Bly (see above, Chapter 1, p. 20).

For the governess, the significance of the figure at the window is that Quint appeared 'with I won't say greater distinctness, for that was impossible, but with a nearness that represented a forward stride in our intercourse' (p. 32). She also becomes convinced that 'it was not for me he had come there. He had come for someone else' (p. 32). But it is only gradually that the full meaning of the scene dawns on her. She is at first concerned to identify the figure she has seen:

Mrs Grose: No one from the village?
Governess: No.
Mrs Grose: A gentleman then?
Governess: No! Indeed no!
Mrs Grose: What was he like?
Governess: His hair was red, close curling, a long pale face, small
                eyes. His look was sharp, fixed and strange. He was
                tall, clean-shaven, yes, even handsome.
                But a horror!
Mrs Grose: Quint! Peter Quint!
                Dear God, is there no end to his dreadful ways?   (I. 5)

It is a perceptive stroke of characterisation that makes Mrs Grose react to the governess's description as being merely a continuation of the dissolute career of the living Quint. (In James she even refers to him in the present tense: 'But he *is* handsome?' (p. 37).) For Mrs Grose, the evil at Bly is in the recent past, and Quint's shortcomings in life seem more to the purpose than his intrinsic repulsiveness as a ghost:

Mrs Grose: . . . Quint was free with everyone – with
little master Miles –
Governess: Miles!
Mrs Grose: Hours they spent together.
Governess: Miles!
Mrs Grose: Yes, Miss, he made free with
her too – with lovely Miss Jessel, governess to those
pets, those angels, those innocent babes – and she
a lady, so far above him.
Dear God! Is there no end!
But he had ways to twist them round his little finger.
He liked them pretty, I can tell you, Miss – and he had
his will, morning and night. (I. 5)

She reveals only gradually, as if it is unimportant, the fact that Quint is dead, and as Lord Harewood has written, 'the colour drains from the orchestra, like blood from the face, as the governess understands she saw a ghost' (Harewood in Kobbé, p. 1492).

In the interchange quoted above, we can see how the governess seizes on the connexion, implied in passing by Mrs Grose, between Quint and Miles. However, Mrs Grose is more concerned to tell the story of Quint and Miss Jessel, which must have impinged more forcibly on her at the time: Miss Jessel's departure from Bly (presumably pregnant by Quint) left the children to Mrs Grose's diffident care – 'And then she went. She couldn't stay, not then. She went away to die' (I. 5). The governess is curiously unmoved by Miss Jessel's fate and instead of drawing parallels between the dead governess and herself, she sees herself in a relationship with Quint. Dismissing any idea that Quint might have been looking for another female victim, she asserts instead, 'He came to look for Miles, I'm sure of that, and he will come again.' She already sees herself and Quint as rivals in a struggle for Miles – which is, of course, what they become.

From this scene onwards her obsession with Miles begins. It is difficult to resist the conclusion that she has transferred her infatuation from the guardian to the boy. It might plausibly be suggested that the transference is the result of the shock of the scene by the tower, when her eager anticipation of meeting the guardian was so horribly repulsed. At all events we have another confusion of identity here. At the opening of the scene, the governess acted out Quint's appearance at the window. Now she adopts the guardian's role – or what she feels his role ought to be – creating a new relationship between herself and the children:

But I see it now, I must protect the children, I must
guard their quiet, and their guardian's too.
See what I see, know what I know, that they may
see and know nothing.   (I. 5)

But although she refers to 'the children' she means Miles. The musical organisation of the opera supports this thesis: up to the end of Act I scene 5 the children are undifferentiated. They are always on stage together and present a composite musical character, singing almost exclusively in canon (Act I scene 2) or unison (Act I scene 3, Act I scene 5). From Act I scene 6 they are sharply individualised. Miles's music in particular has an ambivalence, typified by his 'Malo' song, which allows his most innocent utterances to feed the governess's doubts and suspicions. At the same time he begins to interact less with Flora than with the governess, exercising a fascination over her that ultimately dominates all her thoughts and responses. A committed adherent to the 'second story' might postulate that her subconscious mind created the ghosts in order to give her an excuse to intensify her protective role. It then becomes very significant indeed that it is Quint who is 'raised' first and consequently Miles who receives the full force of her passion. The governess's relationships with Flora and with Miss Jessel lack the intensity, the surely sexual power, of her relations with Miles and Quint.

The Lesson is a scene not directly represented in James. There are passing references to schoolroom life, the most substantial of which hints at both the learning songs and the acting:

They were at this period extravagantly and preternaturally fond of me; which, after all, I could reflect, was no more than a graceful response in children perpetually bowed over and hugged. The homage of which they were so lavish succeeded, in truth, for my nerves, quite as well as if I never appeared to myself, as I may say, literally to catch them at a purpose in it. They had never, I think, wanted to do so many things for their poor protectress; I mean – though they got their lessons better and better, which was naturally what would please her most – in the way of diverting, entertaining, surprising her; reading her passages, telling her stories, acting her charades, pouncing out at her, in disguises, as animals and historical characters, and above all astonishing her by the 'pieces' they had secretly got by heart and could interminably recite. I should never get to the bottom – were I to let myself go even now – of the prodigious private commentary, all under still more private correction, with which, in these days, I overscored their full hours. They had shown me from the first a facility for everything, a general faculty which, taking a fresh start, achieved remarkable flights. They got their little tasks as if they loved them, and indulged, from the mere exuberance of the gift, in the most unimposed little miracles of memory.   (p. 56)

Mrs Piper uses these incidents as James does to juxtapose the governess's suspicions with objective evidence of the children's charm and wholesomeness. A pattern is emerging. The shadow cast by the letter from Miles's school was dispelled by 'Lavender's blue', the appearance on the tower by 'Tom, Tom the Piper's son', and now the terror aroused by Mrs Grose's revelations about Quint is to some extent disarmed by the diligence and normality of the children, as Miles recites his Latin mnemonics and Flora dramatises her history lesson.

James uses the schoolroom scenes to show the governess's perception of a changing relationship with the children: she admits her own idolatry – 'children perpetually bowed over and hugged' – and deduces an 'extravagant' and 'preternatural' response in them. Mrs Piper's scene, too, advances the intimacy between the governess and her charges, but raises questions more specifically than James does about Miles's real character and his relationship with the governess. When she presses the boy to recall more Latin songs, Miles sings what is to become the central expression of his character (see Ex. 1).

Ex. 1

(I. 6)

This song has no source in James and no exact counterpart in the story, but in the opera it becomes a crucial component, embodying in both words and music the poignant ambiguity which surrounds Miles: 'I would rather be. . . in an apple tree. . . than a naughty boy. . . in adversity.' The song gives Miles, for the first time in the opera, his own individualised musical character. Flora never sings 'Malo', and never even echoes its cadences as she did in Miles's earlier music. The only other character to sing it is the governess, and from its first appearance, the song creates a bond between the two of them. It is she who called

this ambivalent expression of his character into being, and her under-
stated reaction prompts Miles to issue the first of his challenges:

Governess: Why, Miles, what a funny song! Did I teach you that?
Miles: No, I found it. I like it. Do you?   (I. 6)

The depths, musical and verbal, of 'Malo' show up the artificial shal-
lows of the earlier nursery games.

The next scene, *The Lake*, aims to raise questions about Flora
which the governess has already answered to her own satisfaction
about Miles. A geography lesson replaces Latin, and Flora rattles off
a catalogue of seas to parallel Miles's mnemonic songs. The counterpart of 'Malo' is the lullaby she sings to her doll:

> Go to sleep, go to sleep!
>
> Dolly must sleep wherever I choose.
> Today by the dead salt sea,
> Tomorrow her waxen lids may close
> On the plains of Muscovy.
>
> And now like a Queen of the East she lies,
> With a Turk to guard her bed,
> But next, when her short-lived daylight dies,
> She's a shepherdess instead.
>
> But sleep dear, dolly, O sleep and when
> You are lost in your journeying dream,
> The sea may change to a palace again,
> For nothing shall stay the same. . .   (I. 7)

Compared with 'Malo' it is lacking in ominous resonances, and as it
is sung in this scene it is the embodiment of innocent imagination.
But when we meet a snatch of it in Act II we are offered the possibility of interpreting it as a spell which lulls Mrs Grose to sleep and
quiets the governess's vigilance for a while.

Flora, then, weaves her spell, and as if in response, Miss Jessel
appears on the other side of the lake. Both James and Mrs Piper
make quite specific the fact that Flora does not see Miss Jessel:

I transferred my eyes straight to little Flora, who, at the moment, was about
ten yards away. My heart had stood still for an instant with the wonder and
terror of the question whether she too would see; and I held my breath while
I waited for what a cry from her, what some sudden innocent sign either of
interest or of alarm, would tell me. I waited, but nothing came; then, in the
first place – and there is something more dire in this, I feel, than in anything
I have to relate – I was determined by a sense that, within a minute, all

sounds from her had previously dropped; and, in the second, by the circumstance that, also within the minute, she had, in her play, turned her back to the water. (p. 44)

She goes on rustling and patting the doll, pulling the coverlet on, arranging reeds over her head. . . she turns round deliberately to face the audience as Miss Jessel appears at the other side of the lake.[10] (I. 7)

The governess however sees her (though in James she is only aware of a presence, as yet unidentified) and the orchestra resounds with the question 'Who is it?' as she hurries Flora away. Once she is alone, the governess expresses her certainty ('It was Miss Jessel', I. 7) and her conviction that both children are aware of the ghosts:

I neither save nor shield them.
I keep nothing from them.

Oh I am useless, useless. What can I do?
It is far worse than I dreamed.

They are lost! Lost! Lost! (I. 7)

One layer of ambiguity is lost when this scene was transferred from book to stage. In James, the governess is aware simply of 'the presence, at a distance, of a third person' (pp. 43–4) and when she tries to rationalise her alarm she reminds herself 'that nothing was more natural. . . than the appearance of one of the men about the place, or even of a messenger, a postman or a tradesman's boy from the village' (p. 44). All these 'possibilities', it will be noted, are male. It is not until she retells the experience to Mrs Grose, dwelling not on the figure but on Flora's alleged awareness of it, that she describes a *female* figure, 'a woman in black, pale and dreadful' (p. 46). We are left to infer that if her possessive passion for Miles has led her to 'raise' the ghost of Quint, then the provision of a counterpart for Flora would inevitably follow. Indeed, so 'natural' does the coupling of Miles with Quint and Flora with Miss Jessel seem to the governess that she is considerably taken aback when, in the last scene of the story, Miles seems to sense the presence of Miss Jessel where she expects him to see Quint:

'No more, no more!' I shrieked, as I tried to press him against me, to my visitant.
'Is she *here*?' Miles panted as he caught with his sealed eyes the direction of my words. Then as his strange 'she' staggered me and, with a gasp, I echoed it, 'Miss Jessel! Miss Jessel!' he with a sudden fury gave me back.
I seized, stupefied, his supposition – some sequel to what we had done to

3 English Music Theatre Company, Snape 1976, Act I scene 8. Iris Saunders, Anthony Rolfe Johnson, Janet Gail, Andrew Harding. Producer Colin Graham, designer Yolanda Sonnabend

Flora, but this made me only want to show him that it was better still than that. 'It's not Miss Jessel! But it's at the window – straight before us. It's *there* – the coward horror, there for the last time!' (pp. 120-1)

In the opera this significant confusion is sacrificed and Miles asks simply, 'Is he there?' The libretto, which has to simplify both words and events, makes the governess's recognition of Miss Jessel in Act I scene 7 immediate too: after all the audience can see a female figure. But Mrs Piper's version manages to retain the all-important sense that the plot is propelled along by the governess's expectations rather than her actual experiences.

The first act culminates in scene 8, *At Night*. The governess discovers Miles and Flora actually communicating with Quint and Miss Jessel, and when questioned by the governess, Miles issues his second challenge: 'You see – I am bad, I am bad, aren't I?' (I. 8). It is interesting to observe how closely this scene, which fulfils the musical and dramatic requirements of an act finale by bringing all the characters on stage together, is modelled on James, in whose story it also forms a turning point. It is crucial, however, to establish whether it retains the essential ambiguities of the story.

The governess has hitherto believed that the ghosts are trying to communicate with the children. At the mid-story climax she has – or thinks she has – proof that the children in their turn initiate communication with the ghosts. But the evidence remains equivocal, for in James the governess finds Flora at the window and Miles on the lawn but does not herself see either ghost. This fact has to be inferred from James's deliberately reticent account. The governess's narration is a blend of exact observation and a wild leaping to conclusions. She finds Flora looking out of the nursery window at night and carefully describes how the child was 'squeezed in behind the blind' (p. 63) – in other words, the blind covered both window and child and the governess had no means of knowing what, if anything, Flora saw. Yet within moments she decides that Flora 'was face to face with the apparition we had met at the lake' (p. 63). To confirm this random guess, she seeks an empty room from which to look out onto the garden. She chooses one (why, unless she was again, as she was in Act I scene 5, compelled to act out Quint's movements?) directly below the tower on which Quint first appeared. Her 'proof', then, is a matter of geometry – of angles. She sees Miles on the lawn, looking 'not so much straight at me as at something that was apparently above me' (p. 64). In the story, therefore, the governess sees neither Miss Jessel nor Quint at this point. The opera, however, stages what she believes to be taking place. It is unfortunate that the visual subtlety of the scene is lost in the interest of audibility: in the opera house the scene is almost always played with the children facing the audience rather than their ghostly interlocutors. The ambiguity of their angles of vision has to be transferred to the words and the music.

Mrs Piper's task was no easy one. 'Britten was determined that [the ghosts] should sing – and sing words (no nice anonymous, supernatural humming or groaning)' (Piper in Herbert (ed.), p. 9). Any words assigned to the ghosts would, of course, make clear the relationship between the ghosts and the children and define the nature of their 'corruption', which is left unspoken in James.

There is a hint in James that the evil that was in Quint arose in the first place out of his passion for power. It has been said that what he actually says to Miles in the opera is laughably lacking in evil. But I felt that the problem was not so much to show him as evil as to suggest what there could be about him that attracted so inexperienced and innocent a child. We had agreed that since the work was to be written in prose, except for the children's rhymes, here was the place for verse, so as to separate the dead, even more, from the living. One of the more obvious ways for evil to present itself to the innocent is in some form of siren song. What Quint sings is an expression of the kind of mystery that could surround a half-known grown-up in the thoughts of a romantic and isolated boy.   (Piper in Herbert (ed.), pp. 11–12)

In the event, the sense of evil is communicated at least as strongly by vocal timbre as by those problematic words. Quint, accompanied by the icy tones of the celesta, sings a melismatic flourish on Miles's name which exploited the special tone quality of Peter Pears's voice (see Ex. 2). Lord Harewood has revealed that this passage 'might never have been put in quite these musical terms if the composer had not heard Peter Pears, the original Quint, singing unaccompanied Perotin. . . in Aldeburgh Church a year or so earlier' (Harewood in Kobbé, p. 1494). The roles written for Pears in all of Britten's operas are set apart from the other vocal writing by their dependence on a specific style of interpretation. Robert Tear, a distinguished successor to Pears in the role of Quint, has suggested that 'in the long run, other voices may not be able to cope with it. . . the technique involved is almost wholly attuned to Britten's music and is difficult to use in other pieces. . . if it is not sung in the Pears fashion, it will sound wrong-headed' (Blyth, p. 155).

Both composer and librettist sought to retain some ambiguity in the scene. It is the governess, not the audience, who is satisfied that the scene provides concrete proof of 'something malign at Bly' (Piper

Ex. 2

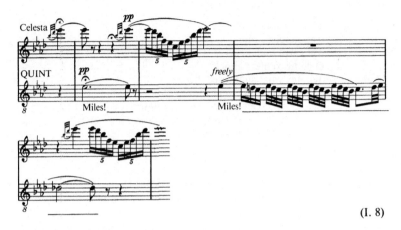

(I. 8)

in Blyth (ed.), p. 82). We are free to believe that she sees what she
expects to see: that the ghostly appearances and their malevolent
blandishments are conjured up in her imagination only. The level of
subtlety in this masterly libretto can be appreciated by realising that
even the children's words do not quite confirm the objective presence
of the ghosts. They, too, can be taken to be projecting imaginative
fantasies. Neither child responds to the evil in the ghosts' words. Miles
seizes on the harmless images suggested by Quint and rejects all the
more pernicious suggestions:

Quint: I'm all things strange and bold,
      The riderless horse,
      Snorting, and stamping on the hard sea sand,
      The hero-highwayman plundering the land.
      I am King Midas with gold in his hand.
Miles: Gold, O yes, gold!
Quint: I am the smooth world's double face,
      Mercury's heels
      Feather'd with mischief and a god's deceit.
      The brittle blandishment of counterfeit.
      In me secrets, and half-formed desires meet.
Miles: Secrets, O secrets!
Quint: I am the hidden life that stirs
      When the candle is out;
      Upstairs and down, the footsteps barely heard.
      The unknown gesture, the soft persistent word,
      The long sighing flight of the night-winged bird.
Miles: Bird!   (I. 8)

Flora, too, picks up the magic enticements of Miss Jessel's complaint and shares no part of her bitterness:

Miss Jessel: Their dreams and ours
               Can never be one,
               They will forsake us.
               O come to me! Come!
Flora: Tell me, what shall I see there?
Miss Jessel: All those we have wept for together;
               Beauty forsaken in the beast's demesne.
               The little mermaid weeping on the sill,
               Gerda and Psyche seeking their loves again,
               Pandora, with her dreadful box, as well.
Flora: Pandora with her box as well!   (I. 8)

The children evince no more than a very normal fascination with night and 'the hidden life that stirs when the candle is out' – the very normality being underlined by Mrs Piper's own account of the genesis of the scene: 'I searched about for possibilities in books and dreams and remembered too being driven as a child into a state of high excitement and frustration by the sounds of adult life after I had gone to bed' (Piper in Herbert (ed.), p. 12).

If we take Act I scene 8 to be a projection of the governess's delusions, then it is no great step to take Act II scene 1, the *Colloquy* between Quint and Miss Jessel, as further evidence of her poisoned imagination. Interestingly enough, early criticism of the opera tended to regard Act I scene 8 as a greater stumbling block to the 'second story' interpretation than Act II scene 1. For example:

[Mrs Piper] has occasionally been insensitive to some of Henry James's silences and reticences, without the one conceivable justification of using a definite interpretation of them. The unhappiest example is the last scene of Act I, in which the episode with Miles on the lawn at night is expanded[11] into a quartet in which the relationship between the children and the ghosts is made crudely explicit, and yet no more intelligible.

On the other hand, her idea of balancing this scene with another at the beginning of Act 2, a duet for the ghosts alone, comes off very convincingly as an imaginative filling out and not a violation of James's silence.

(Colin Mason, *Guardian*, 15 September 1954, p. 5)

In *Colloquy* the ghosts occupy the stage boldly, not separated from the audience by the tower, the lake or the window. They sing, quite explicitly, of a motivation scarcely hinted at in James:

Quint: I seek a friend –
           Obedient to follow where I lead,
           Slick as a juggler's mate to catch my thought,
           Proud, curious, agile, he shall feed

> My mounting power.
> Then to his bright subservience I'll expound
> The desperate passions of a haunted heart. . .

Miss Jessel: I too must have a soul to share my woe.
> Despised, betrayed, unwanted she must go
> Forever to my joyless spirit bound. . .   (II. 1)

And in a particularly bold stroke, Mrs Piper sums up the specific threat offered by Quint and Miss Jessel – the threat to the governess as well as to the children – in a telling quotation from Yeats:

What is absorbing and fascinating about *The Turn of the Screw* is not the sin that lies beneath the fine mist of evil, nor yet the Governess's unfulfilled love, which it was at one time the Freudian fashion to make responsible for the whole affair, but the vulnerability of innocence at all ages. The children's inquiring innocence is assailed from outside, the young woman's is attacked from within by her own fears and imagination and from without by the evidence of her bemused senses, which she constantly mistrusts.

When I discovered the line in W. B. Yeats's poem *The Second Coming* that I used in the Ghosts' colloquy:
> The ceremony of innocence is drowned.
it seemed to epitomize the story; and Britten gave it the theme of the whole work.   (Piper in Herbert (ed.) p. 22)

The second half of the scene is a *Soliloquy* for the governess, and this scene is the closest the libretto comes to opting for the 'second story'. The governess sings, 'Lost in my labyrinth, I see no truth' – which can be read as a denial of the objective reality of the preceding scenes. Echoing the ghosts' words, she declares, 'Innocence, you have corrupted me' and concludes with what might almost be a definition of the second interpretation: 'I know nothing of evil yet I feel it, I fear it, worse – imagine it.' (II. 1).

The second scene of Act II is *The Bells*:

Walking to church a certain Sunday morning, I had little Miles at my side and his sister, in advance of us and at Mrs Grose's, well in sight. It was a crisp, clear day, the first of its order for some time; the night had brought a touch of frost, and the autumn air, bright and sharp, made the church-bells almost gay. It was an odd accident of thought that I should have happened at such a moment to be particularly and very gratefully struck with the obedience of my little charges. Why did they never resent my inexorable, my perpetual society? Something or other had brought nearer home to me that I had all but pinned the boy to my shawl and that, in the way our companions were marshalled before me, I might have appeared to provide against some danger of rebellion. I was like a gaoler with an eye to possible surprises and escapes. But all this belonged – I mean their magnificent little surrender – just to the special array of the facts that were most abysmal. Turned out for Sunday by his uncle's tailor, who had had a free hand and a notion of pretty waistcoats and of his grand little air, Miles's whole title to independence, the rights of his sex and situation, were so stamped upon him that if he had suddenly struck for freedom I should have had nothing to say. I was by the strangest of chances wondering how I should meet him when the revolution unmistakably occurred. I call it a revolution because I now see how, with the word he spoke, the curtain rose on the last act of my dreadful drama and the catastrophe was precipitated. 'Look here, my dear, you know,' he charmingly said, 'when in the world, please, am I going back to school?'   (p. 77)

The scene is closely recreated in the opera, the most significant difference being that Mrs Piper has Flora and Miles entering together, singing their mild distortion of that most parodyable of all the canticles, the *Benedicite*. Consequently, in the opera Miles has to seek out the governess, to linger when Mrs Grose and Flora have already entered the church, in fact to take the initiative in instigating his rebellion. The correspondence between composer and librettist reveals how musical considerations can influence the dramatic structure of a scene, causing discrepancies between the libretto and its source: 'I feel that one must for dramatic and musical reasons have a set piece for the kids at the beginning [of the churchyard scene]' (Britten, quoted in Herbert (ed.), p. 11). Britten conveys the governess's underlying uneasiness in the face of so wholesome a scene by giving the bells, which sound throughout the preceding interlude, an easily-detected variation of the 'Screw theme' (see Chapter 3).

This scene starts a new idea which permeates the second act so significantly that it comes as a shock to realise that Britten and Piper had initially decided 'to leave out the whole episode of the governess's letter to the guardian' (Piper in Herbert (ed.), p. 11). A little scene was transferred from Chapter 12 to Act II scene 2, in which the prospect of writing to the guardian is first proposed:

'Their uncle. . . must take them away.'

   'And who's to make him?'

   She had been scanning the distance, but she now dropped on me a foolish face.'You, Miss.'

   'By writing to him that his house is poisoned and his little nephew and niece mad?'

   'But if they *are*, Miss?'

   'And if I am myself, you mean? That's charming news to be sent him by a governess whose prime undertaking was to give him no worry.'

   Mrs Grose considered, following the children again. 'Yes, he do hate worry.'   (pp. 70–1)

Miles revives the idea when, at the end of the churchyard scene, he urges the governess to take up with his uncle the matter of his going back to school, and tests her with the ambiguous challenge: 'Does

4 Welsh National Opera, Cardiff 1979, Act II scene 2. Cheryl Edwards, David Hubbard. Producer, Adrian Slack; designer, David Fielding.

my uncle think what you think?' (James, p. 80; libretto, II. 2). This letter – the writing of it and what happens to it – is central to the remainder of the opera.

The governess at first rejects Miles's challenge and plans to escape from Bly. (James shows her moderating her initial impulse to leave Bly altogether to a plan to escape for a mere two hours.) Returning to the house (in Act II scene 3, *Miss Jessel*) she finds Miss Jessel seated at her desk in the schoolroom. Forced into direct conflict after so many scenes of tilting at shadows and ambiguities, she realises that she cannot abandon the children ('They are mine, mine'). As the ghost vanishes, the governess takes Miss Jessel's place at the desk (just as in Act I scene 5 she took Quint's place at the window) and writes to the guardian.

The placing of the letter writing at this point (and, indeed, the actual music which accompanies it) is one of the finest inventions in the opera. James delays the writing till the evening of the same day, and then it takes place 'off-stage', with no hints as to the mood of the writer except that she 'sat for a long time before a blank sheet of paper' (p. 87), or more crucially, the actual content beyond that it contained 'the bare demand for an interview' (p. 108). The suggestion, however, for Mrs Piper's scene is obliquely present in James, when the governess returns from church to the schoolroom:

Seated at my own table in the clear noonday light I saw a person whom, without my previous experience, I should have taken at the first blush for some housemaid who might have stayed at home to look after the place and who, availing herself of rare relief from observation and of the schoolroom table and my pens, ink and paper, had applied herself to the considerable effort of a letter to her sweetheart.   (p. 83)

The letter was a milestone for the governess – both an admission of failure and the fulfilment of a cherished fantasy to bring herself again into the presence of the guardian. Some of her inhibitions are sketched in an earlier scene in James:

'You see me asking him for a visit?' No, with her eyes on my face she evidently couldn't. Instead of it even – as a woman reads another – she could see what I myself saw: his derision, his amusement, his contempt for the breakdown of my resignation at being left alone and for the fine machinery I had set in motion to attract his attention to my slighted charms. She didn't know – no one knew – how proud I had been to serve him and to stick to our terms; yet she none the less took the measure, I think, of the warning I now gave her. 'If you should so lose your head as to appeal to him for me–'
    She was really frightened. 'Yes, Miss?'
    'I would leave, on the spot, both him and you.'   (p. 71)

But in Mrs Piper's scene there is no hint of embarrassed pride. The letter is 'written' by the orchestra in a passionate outburst whose content is only defined when the governess reads it over:

Sir – dear sir – my dear sir – I have not forgotten your charge of silence, but there are things that you must know, and I must see and tell you, at once. Forgive me.   (II. 3)

The words are reticent. It is the music which turns the passage into the most tender – and most outspoken – avowal of love from a woman to a man in the whole canon of Britten's operas.

Act II scene 4, *The Bedroom*, is closely based on Chapter 17 of James. Whole sentences of the taut dialogue between Miles and the governess are transferred to the opera, and Mrs Piper arranges them to convey the mounting tension of the scene and its frustrating climax without making any more specific than James does the half-admissions of unease the governess draws from Miles. The presence of Quint, which in the story the governess intuits – '[Miles] waited, he called for guidance. . . It wasn't for *me* to help him – it was for the thing I had met!' (p. 88) – is indicated in the opera by the off-stage voice of Quint:

Miles – are you listening?
Miles – I am here.
Miles – I'm waiting, I'm waiting, waiting, Miles.   (II. 4)

There is a kind of pre-enactment of the last scene of the opera when the governess presses Miles to reject Quint and turn to her:

Miles, if you knew how I want to help you, how I want you to help me save you.   (II. 4)

These words, dangerously revealing in the context of the reticent verbal duel between the two, are accompanied by a smothering embrace. James's description of it again underlines the similarity with the last scene of the story: 'it made me drop on my knees beside the bed and seize once more the chance of possessing him' (p. 90). But on this occasion the governess does not succeed in 'possessing' Miles:

But I knew in a moment. . . that I had gone too far. The answer to my appeal was instantaneous, but it came in the form of an extraordinary blast and chill, a gust of frozen air and a shake of the room as great as if, in the wild wind, the casement had crashed in. The boy gave a loud, high shriek which, lost in the rest of the shock of sound, might have seemed, indistinctly, though I was so close to him, a note either of jubilation or of terror. I jumped to my feet again and was conscious of darkness. So for a moment we

remained, while I stared about me and saw that the drawn curtains were unstirred and the window tight. 'Why, the candle's out!' I then cried.
'It was I who blew it, dear!' said Miles.   (p. 91)

In Variation XII and Act II scene 5, which flow together as a single scene, Quint successfully tempts Miles to steal the governess's letter. Miles's theft of the letter is one of the two items of objective evidence of Miles's 'evil' propensities in the opera (the other is his expulsion from school) though the real evil is perhaps less in Miles's actions than in the governess's over-reaction to both events.

Act II scene 6, *The Piano*, shares with Act I scene 4, *The Tower*, and Act II scene 2, *The Bells*, an aural inspiration from James. Miles entertains the governess with his piano playing. The description of his accomplishment in James is unspecific – 'he sat down at the old piano and played as he had never played' (p. 92) – but there are enough accounts of Miles's precocity in other areas, throughout the story, to render this virtuoso display in character.

The scene deals with enchantment, and the ambiguity lies in what it is that enchants us – either it is the spell that any child can cast at any time over a warmly prejudiced audience, or we may believe it to be the deliberate sorcery of Miles's piano playing and Flora's game of 'cat's cradle' which ensnares the governess and Mrs Grose. The introduction of Flora and Mrs Grose into the scene is an invention of Mrs Piper's, enabling her to quote briefly from Flora's spell song in Act I scene 7 and to transform that lullaby retrospectively into a spell. For the governess, the scene is evidence of collusion between the children: 'He's found the most divine little way to keep me quiet while she went' (II. 6). And in James, when Mrs Grose echoes her 'divine', the governess retorts, 'Infernal, then!' (p. 94). Her confidence has grown to the pitch where she no longer questions what she sees or hesitates to draw conclusions. She is ready to interpret any incident as evidence of the children's 'possession' and, in deducing a collaboration between Miles and Flora in this scene, she shows that she is now as certain about scenes she has not witnessed as about those she has.

Her growing conviction is reflected in the accelerating momentum of the drama. In Act I all the interludes represent some passage of time, the spacing out of the 'drops' and 'flights' and the selection of significant incidents from the 'long months when nothing and everything happened' (see above, p. 28). In Act II several of the scenes are run together. There is continuous action from Act II scene 2 through Variation X to Act II scene 3; Act II scene 4, Variation XI and Act II

5 Royal Theatre Copenhagen, 1967, Act II Variation XII. Kurt Westi, Svend
Eric Larsen. Producer, Geoffrey Connor; designer, Dacre Punt.

scene 5 make another sequence; similarly Act II scene 6, Variation XII and Act II scene 7.

In Variation XII we hear Miles still at the piano, playing, the governess believes, a triumphant celebration of the success of his 'infernal' plot. By the opening of Act II scene 7, Mrs Grose and the governess have reached the lake (in James we are told that ever since the incident in Act I scene 7 the governess had prevented Flora from visiting it) and find Flora there, alone. Mrs Grose fusses round her: 'Fancy running off like that, and such a long way, too, without your hat and coat.' But the governess, armed with her new certainty, asks Flora the direct question whose counterpart she was unable to bring herself to pronounce in Act II scene 4: 'And where, my pet, is Miss Jessel?'

Immediately Miss Jessel appears on the opposite side of the lake, summoned into being, it would seem, by the governess's accusation. It is the first time one of the ghosts has appeared in the presence of Mrs Grose and she sees – nothing. Earlier in the opera, this lack of corroboration would have shaken the governess. It has no effect on her now, except to provoke her continued assertions: 'Only look, dearest woman, don't you see, Now! Now!. . . But look!' Flora reacts hysterically:

I can't see anybody, can't see anything, nobody, nothing, nobody, nothing; I don't know what you mean.

She then turns to denounce the governess and we get a mild enough hint of the verbal abuse which later shocks Mrs Grose into believing in Flora's corruption:

You're cruel, horrible, hateful, nasty, Why did you come here?

Mrs Piper's handling of the ghosts was severely criticised by some reviewers when the opera first appeared. The critic of *The Times* found that 'Quint and Miss Jessel behave like two too solid stage villains' (*The Times*, 16 September 1954, p. 9). Martin Cooper claimed that the ghosts 'appear too often. . . and say too much' (*Daily Telegraph*, 15 September 1954, p. 8), and Reginald Smith Brindle (*Observer*, 19 September 1954, p. 15) also felt that the essential ambiguities in James were obscured by the 'all too concrete' ghosts. Such criticism, however, seems to overlook the effect of this scene. Here the audience sees Miss Jessel and hears her sing, but they also see that the governess sees her and that both Flora and Mrs Grose look in her direction but deny her presence. The scene, then, forms the strongest possible evidence for the 'second story' implicit in James. Mrs Grose's stolid denials –

6 Royal Theatre Copenhagen, 1967, Act II scene 7. Bonna Sondberg, Else Margrete Gardelli, Ellen Margrethe Edlers, Grith Fjeldmose. Producer, Geoffrey Connor; designer, Dacre Punt.

She isn't there.
Why, poor Miss Jessel's dead and buried, we know that, love.

– force the audience to question the governess's sanity as they have
never questioned it before. And Mrs Piper points up the 'second
story' even more clearly when the governess realises that Flora's
stream of abuse is directed at herself:

Flora (pointing at the governess): I don't like her!
                                       I hate her!
Governess (with horror):   Me!

The scene ends with a bewildered Mrs Grose leading Flora back to
the house. Miss Jessel disappears and the governess is left alone with
an overwhelming sense of failure:

Flora, I have lost you.
She has taught you how to hate me.
. . . I have failed, failed, most miserably
failed, and there is no more innocence in me.

Mrs Grose's support, however, is not withheld for long. Act II
scene 8 opens with her acknowledgement of Flora's loss of innocence: 'O Miss, you were quite right, I must take her away. Such a
night as I have spent – No, don't ask me. What that child has poured
out in her dreams – things I never knew nor hope to know, nor dare
remember' (II. 8). The story sheds a little more light on Flora's
outpourings:

'You mean that, since yesterday, you *have* seen – ?'
    She shook her head with dignity. 'I've *heard* – !'
'Heard?'
    'From that child – horrors! There.' she sighed with tragic relief. 'On my
honour, Miss, she says things – !' But at this evocation she broke down; she
dropped, with a sudden sob, upon my sofa and, as I had seen her do before,
gave way to all the grief of it.
    It was in quite another manner that I, for my part, let myself go. 'Oh,
thank God!'
    She sprang up again at this, drying her eyes with a groan. '"Thank God?"'
'It so justifies me!'
'It does that, Miss!'
    I couldn't have desired more emphasis, but I just hesitated. 'She's so
horrible?'
    I saw my colleague scarce knew how to put it. 'Really shocking.'
'And about me?'
    'About you, Miss – since you must have it. It's beyond everything, for a
young lady; and I can't think wherever she must have picked up – '
    'The appalling language she applied to me? I can, then!' I broke in with a
laugh that was doubtless significant enough.
    It only, in truth, left my friend still more grave. 'Well, perhaps I ought to
also – since I've heard some of it before!'   (pp. 106–7)

This does not, of course, constitute objective proof that Flora has been corrupted by supernatural spirits. It does not take a ghost to teach a child to swear, any more than it takes one to teach theft. Flora's 'appalling language' could as well have been learnt from the living Quint, through Miles, as from communication with the shade of Miss Jessel. The governess, however, has long since ceased to probe the 'evidence' of the children's 'corruption', and Mrs Grose is too shocked by Flora's outburst to examine the facts rationally. She herself supplies the next testimony against the children: 'My dear, your letter never went, it wasn't where you put it. . . Miles must have taken it' (II. 8).

At this point James shows Mrs Grose leaping to the conclusion that stealing letters must have been the cause of Miles's expulsion from school. It is she, now, rather than the governess, who leads the way in finding new evidence of the children's consistent malefaction: 'I faced her for a moment with a sad smile. "It strikes me that by this time your eyes are open wider than mine"' (p. 108). Adherents to the 'second story' must add Mrs Grose to the catalogue of the governess's victims.

Mrs Grose and Flora leave Bly for London and the final confrontation between the governess and Miles takes place in an intensification of the loneliness and isolation which underlie the entire opera. The dramatic significance of the final scene is supported by a musical structure which matches the denouement with its own autonomous logic, besides colouring the tensions on stage. The musical effect of this scene is discussed in Chapter 3, and for the moment we need only note that it is a passacaglia based on the Screw theme, the principal theme of the opera, which is arrived at cumulatively; extra notes are added to the passacaglia bass to mark crucial stages in the drama. The first section of the finale is worked over the first six notes of the theme.

The libretto follows James closely. The one major difference is that Mrs Piper placed this scene in the grounds of Bly, perhaps to avoid a scene-change after Mrs Grose and Flora's departure, perhaps to make a striking use of the tower for Quint's final appearance. It is, however, now almost always produced as an interior scene. The window (see above, p. 31) has become as potent a symbol as the tower, and James focuses his creation of unease and suspense on Miles's awareness of this:

He faced to the window again and presently reached it with his vague, restless, cogitating step. He remained there a while, with his forehead against the glass, in contemplation of the stupid shrubs I knew and the dull things of November. . . The frames and squares of the great window were a kind of image, for him, of a kind of failure. I felt that I saw him, at any rate, shut in or shut out. He was admirable, but not comfortable: I took it in with a throb of hope. Wasn't he looking through the haunted pane, for something he couldn't see? – and wasn't it the first time in the whole business that he had known such a lapse?   (p. 113)

The governess is determined to confront Miles as she confronted Flora in Act II scene 7. But she cannot bring herself to be quite as direct (perhaps she shrinks from provoking the storm of abuse Flora directed at her) and in any case her relationship with Miles is more subtle. James gives one surprisingly outspoken hint about their relationship in this scene:

We continued silent while the maid was with us – as silent, it whimsically occurred to me, as some young couple who, on their wedding-journey, at the inn, feel shy in the presence of the waiter.   (p. 112)

Mrs Piper takes the hint, and it is a newly sophisticated Miles who initiates the dialogue and traps the governess into admitting more of her ambivalent feelings than she realises:

Miles: So, my dear, we are alone.
Governess: Are we alone?
Miles: O, I'm afraid so.
Governess: Do you mind? do you mind being left alone?
Miles: Do you?
Governess: Dearest Miles, I love to be with you – what else should I stay for?

The governess presses Miles to 'tell me what it is then you have on your mind' (II. 8) and immediately the voice of Quint, off-stage, repeats his seductive call we first heard in Act I scene 8.[12] It is both an answer to her plea – an admission that Quint is precisely what Miles has on his mind – and a revelation of what the governess has on hers. That the entry of Quint's voice marks a new stage in the finale is underlined by the fact that the passacaglia theme is extended to include two more notes. It continues over these eight notes while Miles still manages to evade the governess's questions: 'I will tell you everything. . . But not now' (II. 8). At the climax of this passage Quint appears (on the tower in the original version, at the window in most subsequent productions) but the governess holds Miles so that he cannot see the apparition.

   Her treatment of Miles in this confrontation is in marked contrast to her behaviour towards Flora in the previous scene. In Act II scene 7 she forced Flora to face Miss Jessel:

Look, she is there! (*pointing*)
Look, you little unhappy thing! (II. 7)

Now she 'pushes Miles around so that he can't see [Quint]' (libretto, II. 8). The action is on the surface an intensification of her protective role – she is still concerned to shield Miles from Quint – but it also betrays her possessive fear of competition. She is afraid that if Miles sees Quint he may choose Quint rather than herself. There are sexual resonances in her action too. And there is more than a hint of a woman quizzing her lover over his previous attachments in the interrrogation which follows:

Miles, dear little Miles, who is it you see? Who do you wait for, watch for? . . . who is it, who? Say – for my sake!

This section of the finale was originally intended to be the climax.[13] The last four notes of the passacaglia theme are added to underline Quint's words – 'Do not betray our secrets. . . Miles, you are mine! . . . Don't betray us, Miles!' (II. 8). Simultaneously, Miles is pressed by the governess to name Quint:

Miles: Is he there, is he there?
Governess: Is who there, Miles? Say it! (II. 8)

In the earlier version of this scene, Miles yields at this point and names Quint. But in the final revision, Miles cries out, 'Nobody! Nothing!' (echoing Flora in Act II scene 7) so that the tension is further prolonged.

The last stage of the finale, which takes place over a full statement of the passacaglia theme, focuses not on the duel between Miles and the governess but on that between the governess and Quint. Quint makes his final bid for Miles. He returns to his evocative suggestions in Act I scene 8: 'On the paths, in the woods, remember Quint!' At the same time, the governess persists with her relentless questioning: 'Who made you take the letter?. . . Who do you wait for, watch for?. . . Only say the name and he will go for ever. . .' (II. 8).

The climax is fully as ambiguous in the opera as it is in James. Miles exclaims 'Peter Quint, you devil!', answering neither one nor the other. It is for the producer to determine to whom those last words are addressed. (But see Chapter 4, p. 142.) In such a significant situation we are forced to snatch at the slenderest hints for a final clue to their interpretation. There is a change of punctuation between the two versions which should be noted, though it is not clear that it signals a lesser degree of equivocation. The earlier score which Mitchell quotes (see note 13) has 'Peter Quint! You Devil!' The final version, 'Peter Quint, you devil!' (and James's 'Peter Quint – you devil!') indicates at least that the whole phrase is addressed to one person – but which of the two is still not determined. The libretto's stage directions, '[Miles] runs into the Governess's arms', might be thought to be decisive, but this, too, is an ambiguous action and can be taken as either refuge or attack at the choice of the producer.

Quint disappears as the governess clings to Miles and both sing words which are poignantly ironic:

Quint: Ah Miles, we have failed. . .
Governess: Ah Miles, you are saved, now all will be well.
            Together we have destroyed him.

As the governess realises that the boy is dead she breaks into an impassioned reminiscence of Miles's song: 'Malo than a naughty boy. . . Malo in adversity'. It has never sounded so unambiguously innocent. Her final question 'What have we done between us?' articulates the intrinsic enigma.

3 Benjamin Britten's 'The Turn of the Screw': the music

I The sketches: chronology and analysis

JOHN EVANS

Shortly after embarking on the composition sketch for the Coronation opera, *Gloriana*, in the autumn of 1952, Britten received a commission from the Venice Biennale Festival for a chamber opera which would receive its première at the Fenice theatre in 1954. Encouraged by Peter Pears, Britten was considering Henry James's novella, *The Turn of the Screw*. Myfanwy Piper had suggested the same subject some years earlier, when Britten was toying with the idea of accepting a film offer, so he asked her to propose ways in which the novella might now be adapted for an opera. At this stage William Plomer, the librettist of *Gloriana*, was to have taken over the writing of the text; in the event Myfanwy Piper's proposals were so convincing that Britten entrusted the writing of the libretto to her. However, it would be almost a year before they could proceed with serious work on the text.

In the autumn of 1953, when the final scenario for *The Turn of the Screw* was agreed upon, Britten was taken ill with an acute attack of bursitis in his right shoulder and was forced to cancel all conducting and recital engagements. By the time he had begun receiving the draft libretto from Myfanwy Piper in January 1954 his physical condition was such that his early letters to her were written with his left hand. In March he underwent minor surgery. Now being faced with an extremely tight schedule (if the opera was to be premièred in September 1954 as arranged), Britten began the composition sketch for *The Turn of the Screw* on 30 March, again writing with his left hand. As he completed each scene, further minor revisions to the libretto, as it was being set, were sent to Myfanwy Piper for her approval.

The writing of *The Turn of the Screw*, from composition sketch to manuscript full score, was the result of four intensive months of work from the very end of March to the beginning of August, with Britten devoting most of June to his various commitments during the Aldeburgh Festival. When free to compose, Britten worked at his desk in the morning and late afternoon of each day, finishing each session with a play-through at the piano to review the work as it progressed. The composition sketch for *The Turn of the Screw* is in pencil on eighteen-stave bifolia (with some twenty-stave also) measuring 36.5 × 27 cm.[1] As was the case with all Britten's operas, he sketched in short score with separate staves for each of the solo vocal lines and with an empty stave separating the voice parts from the orchestral reduction. One receives a very strong impression of the orchestral sonorities from the precise details of instrumentation that are found in almost every system of the 155 pages of the composition sketch; Britten committed notes to paper with a vivid sense of the instruments (and, for that matter, the voices) that were to bring them to life. In fact, in almost every respect the composition sketch for *The Turn of the Screw* closely resembles the appearance of the published vocal score,[2] even down to the detailed stage directions. But what distinguishes the sketch from the published score is, of course, the extraordinary fluency of the composer's calligraphy, the occasional traces of unrevised text, and the few deletions, revisions, erasures or inserted replacement folios. Britten's habit was to work always in pencil; changes during the course of composition were most often made by erasure and rewriting. If a complete system did not proceed to his satisfaction this would be crossed out and a second attempt made which, more often than not, came out right. More substantial revisions might necessitate the discarding of a folio, or sometimes a bifolium, and the insertion of a replacement. As each scene or variation was completed, Imogen Holst (who had come to work for Britten as his amanuensis in September 1952, just as he was beginning the composition of *Gloriana*) made a vocal score that could be reproduced by the publishers so that the singers could begin to prepare their roles. As she was later to recall:

The music of *The Turn of the Screw* was written with very little time to spare. I had to copy out the vocal score straight away in batches of half a dozen pages at a time and post them to London the same day. It seemed incredible that a composer could be so sure of what he wanted that he would risk parting with the beginning of a scene before he had written the end of it.[3]

By 12 April Britten had completed the first three scenes of Act I and in a letter to Myfanwy Piper he raised the first of what she herself has described as 'bombshells':[4]

It has been lovely having Basil [Coleman][5] here, we have done a lot of work together on the piece. We have had one major discussion which he will talk to you about. It arose out of a sudden fear that the work is going to be much too short. The first three scenes incidentally play only ten minutes. Please do not be shocked at his suggestion and give it a fair chance. . . it has been in my head for some time. . . a prologue?. . . the interview or the ghost story party? probably spoken?

Having reached the beginning of scene 5 (*The Window*) on 23 April, Britten required a more complete description for the governess of Quint's appearance than Myfanwy Piper had provided in her text. But Britten here solved the problem by suggesting the lines (beginning 'His hair was red, close-curling') which are derived from dialogue in James's story.

By early May Britten had completed Act I and on the 16th he visited Myfanwy Piper at Fawley[6] to work on the final shape of Act II, for which two problems remained. The first of these was a difficulty over the opening of the churchyard scene (*The Bells*), which was only resolved when a clergyman friend of the librettist's suggested using the *Benedicite* for the children's 'gentle make-believe of a choir procession'.[7] Also, the episode of the governess's letter to the children's guardian, which was omitted in the original scheme for Act II, was now found to be essential to the dramatic sequence and was thus reinstated. The question of the *Prologue* was still unresolved and was to remain so until both the composition sketch and full score were completed.

The way in which the manuscript full score was compiled is also typical of Britten's usual working practice. Imogen Holst prepared the twenty-four-stave manuscript paper (measuring 35.5 × 26 cm),[8] in ink, spacing the bar lines, filling in clefs and signatures and writing in the vocal lines. Britten would then fill in the instrumental texture in pencil. There were no revisions at this stage, save for the addition of the *Prologue*. Though work had gone speedily in July, Imogen Holst was still copying out the orchestral parts up to twenty minutes before the first orchestral rehearsal on 2 August.[9] Furthermore, this schedule left no time for the publishers to prepare a conducting score for Britten to use for the first performance, and the restricted lighting in the orchestral pit at the Fenice theatre in Venice would have proved insufficient to have made the pencilled parts of the manuscript full score legible. At Britten's request, Imogen Holst therefore inked in over Britten's writing in pencil throughout the score. The result is not fully characteristic of either hand and, for the want of a better word, gives a ghostly appearance to the manuscript.

The revisions undertaken during the writing of *The Turn of the Screw* are reflected not only in the rewritings of the composition sketch, but to an even greater extent in the thirty-one pages of discarded sketches from the manuscript. These are either actual folios discarded from the composition sketch or individual pages of manuscript which bear sketches of themes or textures in an embryonic state.

The process of agreeing on a suitable shape for the *Prologue* was not easy. For instance, Myfanwy Piper, in response to Britten's letter of 12 April, had offered a dramatisation of the introductory ghost-story party from the novella (see Chapter 2, p. 25), but it was decided that this would set quite a different atmosphere from that of the rest of the drama and would prove intrusive. Britten then requested a shorter version of her first proposal, in which a narrator-like character sets the scene for the drama, thus enabling the composer to 'start with a few loud chords and set it naturally as recitative'.[10] Britten's first, discarded attempt at setting the *Prologue* text is much drier than the lyric-recitative setting as we know it. The harmonic support is generally more static; repeated pitches in the voice part are often punctuated by strumming repeated harmonies in the piano accompaniment. Very occasionally the vocal writing takes on the more animated lyrical quality of the finished sketch, notably through the shape of the lines: 'There had been a governess, but she had gone' and 'He was so much engaged – affairs, travel, friends, visits'. The second stage in the setting of the *Prologue* is that found in the composition sketch itself, though even here there are revisions to note. Persisting from the discarded sketch are three 'Introductory Knocks' that were to have preceded the opening music of the *Prologue*. This gesture is borrowed from the conventions of the theatre on the Continent, notably in France, and was originally designed to arrest the attention of the audience. Though this was considered to be necessary at the Fenice, particularly as the opera starts with solo piano, it was a notion that was later abandoned when the production returned to England. The dovetailing of the *Prologue* into the twelve-note theme of the opera (the 'Screw theme') understandably required some refixing in the composition sketch, and the passage immediately preceding the link was somewhat revised. One particular phrase, 'O, he was persuasive', was, at first, highlighted with a melismatic setting, twice repeated and elaborated (see Ex. 3). This had originally sufficed to link '. . . and do her best' with the dovetail into the Screw theme, 'At last "I will," she said'. The eight bars that were

Ex. 3

O   he   was   per-sua-sive   He was per - sua - - - sive

He   was   per - sua - - - - - - sive

inserted at this point serve to underline the image of the young innocent girl becoming rather infatuated by the handsome guardian:

She was full of doubts.
But she was carried away:
that he, so gallant and handsome,
so deep in the busy world, should need her help.

In scene 2 (*The Welcome*) Mrs Grose was originally assigned the
legato line in the ensemble at fig. 10[11] in the score, moving at twice
the speed (i.e. in crotchets rather than minims). Having sketched five
bars of this on one system (without text or vocal counterpoint) the
entire system is deleted and the duet is sketched, without further
amendments, from the following system onwards.

For Variation III (which in its final form is set in D major) Britten
had originally sketched a slow B minor interlude based on a 5/4
ground derived from the first four pitches of the opera's principal
theme (see below, p. 73). Pitches five to eight then shadow the ground
at the quaver over which the original dotted rhythmic guise of the
Screw theme is restored for pitches nine to twelve (see Ex. 4).

Ex. 4

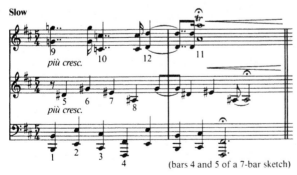

(bars 4 and 5 of a 7-bar sketch)

With the series now complete and poised on a trill on A (the order of the last two pitches, A and D, having been reversed) the variation moves into a variant of the music from fig 1 that had prepared for the governess's journey to Bly in scene 1. Though suitably mysterious in tone, and effective in its reprise of musico-dramatically crucial music from scene 1, this variation pales by comparison with the sheer beauty and invention of the subtle evocation of the park at Bly on a summer evening which was to replace it as Variation III (see below, pp. 76–80). While the discarded variation anticipates the disturbing presence of Quint in atmosphere, if not in motif, the tranquil, alfresco setting of Variation III establishes a vivid contrast to the unearthly tones of the celesta that arrest our attention at the moment of Quint's manifestation on the tower.

Variation V, the fugal interlude which precedes scene 6 (*The Lesson*), is written on three separate sheets of manuscript paper which are inserted into the composition sketch, not because the music replaced an earlier draft but because it was written in isolation from the composition sketch itself. The composer's calligraphy is also inferior on these pages. Imogen Holst explains: 'The thirteen-part fugue in *The Turn of the Screw* was written [in a train] between Ipswich and Liverpool Street [London], and for once his very clear manuscript was quite difficult to decipher.'[12]

Both an isolated sketch and a discarded folio exist for Miles's poignant 'Malo' song for scene 6 (*The Lesson*). (See Chapter 2, p. 41). Though the harp's realisation of the harmony is absent from these sketches, the resonant aural images of the viola (the instrument that articulates the apprentice's grief in *Peter Grimes*) and the cor anglais (the plangent tones of which Britten had exploited for the funeral march in his incidental music for *Timon of Athens* (1935) and for Lucretia's final entrance in *The Rape of Lucretia*) are clearly indicated. Notably both sketches are in E minor rather than F minor (as at fig. 51). Though the E minor tonality of the shorter sketch is not in itself extraordinary (when noting ideas for a work, as in the case of the extensive sketch book for *Death in Venice*, for instance, Britten often used keys other than those in which themes would eventually appear) it is clear from the discarded folio that E minor was seriously considered as appropriate to the 'Malo' song. The reworked F minor setting is obviously more logical in relation to the F *major* context of scene 6. But to my mind the decisive factor that influenced the F minor setting of 'Malo' is that it places it in the relative minor of the A♭ major through which the ghosts of Quint and Miss Jessel make contact with the children in scene 8 (*At Night*).

Variation VI and the opening sequence up to fig. 58 of scene 7 (*The Lake*) underwent extensive revision, and, in all, there are eleven pages of discarded sketches for this passage. In the earliest sketches the string *pizzicato* quavers that underpin the arpeggiated wind textures are totally absent and the wind arpeggios establish a predominant texture. Beneath this the Screw theme emerges in slow moving octaves for *pizzicato* double-basses reinforced by bass drum. The process of revision through these sketches is gradual: slowly the string ostinato begins to infiltrate the texture and the wind arpeggios gradually give way to and are articulated by a development of the 'Malo' song.

Various small revisions were made to scene 8 (*At Night*), notably to the end of the duet for Quint and Miss Jessel ('On the paths, in the woods'), in order to prepare for the climax of the phrase on Miss Jessel's top B♭ for 'I shall be there!' The full ensemble at fig. 87 required some revision, the contrapuntal strands of soprano voices in close proximity, underpinned by Quint's haunting refrain, needing some attention before Britten was fully satisfied. The five bars preceding fig. 89 were also much revised: the problem would seem to have been a need to give the strongest shape possible to the governess's little cadenza-like outburst, 'Miles! What are you doing here?' (see Ex. 5).

On the verso of the title page for Act II, facing the composition-sketch for the opening of Variation VIII, Britten has noted two transpositions of the twelve-note theme of the opera, on F and on A♭

Ex. 5

i

What — are you do-ing here?

ii

[Miles _____ what are you do-ing here _____ ?]

iii

Miles! _ what are you do-ing here _____?

(the roots of the relative minor and major modes of the four-flat key signatures of the end of Act I and the start of Act II). To the A♭ series Britten assigns a different instrument to each of the twelve pitches; the instrumental cadenzas of Variation VIII adopt this series and its instrumental allocation (though oboe and clarinet exchange positions). In the first scene of Act II (*Colloquy and Soliloquy*) a four-bar orchestral link from the governess's 'labyrinth' aria into Variation IX was deleted in the composition sketch, thereby dovetailing aria and interlude.

A sixteen-bar discarded sketch for Variation XIV lacks the contrapuntal play between piano and orchestra characteristic of this toccata in its final form. Also related to this variation is a twelve-note series on the verso of one of the sketch pages of the 'Malo' song. Though on B♭, the root of Variation XIV, this series had been worked out in inversion by Britten. However, in the event he decided against adopting this inversion, and both the discarded sketch and the toccata in its final form are constructed on the B♭ series in its original state.

Undoubtedly the most significant and substantial revisions in the entire opera were made to the very last scene (*Miles*). Donald Mitchell discovered this in 1963 when, by chance, he came across a dyeline copy of Imogen Holst's original manuscript vocal score and observed that the music from fig. 130 to the end of the opera was substantially different from that in the published vocal score. In fact Britten had revised the end of the opera when scoring the final scene. The most remarkable aspect of that revision was the insertion of the duet for Quint and the governess at fig. 131, which delays the climax of the scene and most brilliantly combines Quint's alluring song from the end of Act I ('On the paths, in the woods') with the governess's persistent interrogation of Miles ('Who made you take the letter?'). Quint is poised on a characteristic 'black-note' tonal region of A♭, while the governess is overwhelmed by the twelve-note Screw theme in its original rhythmic and tonal guise, on A. Thus the 'white-note–black-note', A–A♭ conflict embodied within the opera's principal theme is intensified within this ensemble at the climax of the passacaglia at the end of the opera (see Ex. 6).[13]

The transition from this duet into the governess's intense reprise of 'Malo' was also revised, and went through three distinct stages. The first of these belongs to the unrevised passage at fig. 131. After the governess's 'Who is it? Tell me. Say it!' and Miles's chilling shriek, 'Peter Quint! You Devil!' (compare Chapter 2, p. 61), a de-

Ex. 6

scending sequence of tremolo chords leads directly into the governess's 'What have we done between us?' (i.e. the music between
figs. 134 and 138 is totally absent). The governess's version of 'Malo'
then begins at the lower octave on E – marked '*pp* As before (in
Act I) "hesitating"' – and builds to a central climax, dying away
towards the curtain. The second stage of this final revision unites
Quint and the governess as at fig. 134 but both strands of the duet
are greatly influenced by a melismatic version of the 'ceremony of
innocence' motif. As in the first sketch, the governess's crucial line,
'Together we have destroyed him', is absent, though the transition
from cor anglais, harp and tremolo strings at fig. 136 to an impassioned reprise of 'Malo', *forte* and on a top F♯, at fig. 137 is now taking shape. The third sketch takes the passage from fig. 134 to fig. 136
a stage further towards its final form, with just a few traces of unrevised text and over-elaborate melisma in the Quint–governess duet
after fig. 134 yet to be ironed out. As Donald Mitchell observes in his
sharply perceptive analysis of Britten's last thoughts on this score,
the revisions to the final scene offer examples of 'intensification
by means of expansion' and 'intensification by means of com-
pression'.[14]

II Structures: an overall view

PATRICIA HOWARD

One of the severest criticisms levelled against *The Turn of the Screw*
by a distinguished reviewer of the first performance was that the
music merely 'set' the libretto, without illuminating and interpreting
the drama through its own structures and expressive tensions. (See
Chapter 4, pp. 134–5.) It is a grotesquely inappropriate assessment,
suggested by the lack of substantial passages of instrumental music,
the deceptively representational function of such instrumental interludes as there are, and the pervasive lyricism of the vocal lines. In
fact *The Turn of the Screw* is Britten's most tightly organised opera,

and it is unique among his dramatic oeuvre in having a self-sufficient musical form which parallels and illuminates the structure of the unfolding story. In Chapter 2 we examined the dramatic form, the unusual episodic construction dictated not only by the form of James's story, but by the subject matter itself – the 'flights and drops' of the governess's experiences, the evidence for and against the objective presence of 'something malign at Bly'. Over and above this, the opera has an autonomous *musical* structure: it is a theme and variations in a wider sense than the series of interludes between the scenes implies. The variation form embraces the entire opera, and there is no absolute division of function, variational and non-variational, between the scenes and the interludes.

Much of the opera's impact – its concentration and intensity – results from the reciprocal relationship between the independent but simultaneously enunciated musical and dramatic structures. The conflict of interest between music and drama is old as opera itself, but in this work the priorities fluctuate: the drama dictates the music when the incidents of the plot require the interludes to act as tone poems, evoking a mood or painting a scene. But these demands do not lessen the musical coherence of the interludes, which advance the musical argument of the opera by manipulating the principal theme in a scheme of cumulative tension. And at the end of the opera, the music dictates the drama by controlling the denouement with the deliberate and inevitable pacing of one of the most tightly organised of all musical structures, the passacaglia. Occasionally the story prescribes the use of specific tone colours or figurations: the bells in Act II scene 2 suggest both the orchestration and the method of treating the theme in the preceding variation,[15] while Miles's piano playing in Act II scene 6 is both crucial to the story – to the governess's assessment of the boy as an active agent for evil – and also provides the starting point for the musical content of Variation XIII, Act II scene 6, and Variation XIV.

The musical structure originates with the statement of a theme which generates nearly two hours of musical development. This theme is so rich, so prolific, in suggestion, that all the characters draw on it to express personalities which range from unambiguous innocence (Mrs Grose is the only candidate here, and the opening of Act II scene 8 questions even her integrity) to depravity. The drama is inevitably affected by the fact that all the important musical material derives from the one theme. This fact is in itself an interpretation of the story: when the governess expresses her intention to *protect* the children in notes almost identical to those Quint uses to *corrupt* them, then the purely musical structure of the opera can be shown to play a part in sustaining and deepening the intrinsic ambiguities of the plot.

In a letter to Myfanwy Piper discussing her suggestions for the title of the opera, Britten wrote, 'I must confess that I have a sneaking, horrid feeling that the original H. J. title describes the musical plan of the work exactly!!' (Headington, p. 111). The theme of the opera is usually referred to as the Screw theme[16] both because of its eponymous structural role and its powerful delineation of mounting tension. It appears immediately after the *Prologue* and was originally planned to be the opening of the opera (see above, p. 25). It was perhaps this placing which suggested the incisive double-dotted rhythm with its long-standing associations with French opera overtures – compare the proposed 'Introductory Knocks' of French theatre tradition John Evans refers to on p. 66. The theme is stated on the piano, but each note is sustained by one of the other instruments as it appears, so that by the final bar all twelve notes are sounding simultaneously (see Ex. 7).

Ex. 7

The theme has a number of easily perceived characteristics which aid its recognition throughout the opera. The rhythm of the initial statement reappears only intermittently. It is, however, conspicuous on the only two occasions in the opera when the theme is sung: the declaration of evil by the ghosts in Act II scene 1 and during the governess's final duet with Quint in Act II scene 8. The melodic structure is far more widely used. Shorn of its movement through three octaves, it resolves into the patterns shown in Ex. 8, which can be further reduced to the circular scheme shown in Ex. 9. It has frequently been pointed out[17] that this is a twelve-note theme which is treated entirely within traditional tonality. That is to say, a tonic is

Ex. 8

Ex. 9

almost always discernible, though the chords which support it are by no means always traditional triads. Even when the tonal centre is obscured by a texture in which all twelve notes are sounded together, a sense of tonic is usually imposed by the melodic movement, as in bars 7–9 of the theme. Britten had often expressed a dissatisfaction with strict serialism and the atonality it implies: 'I am seriously disturbed by its limitations. I can see it taking no part in the music-lover's music-making. Its methods make writing *gratefully* for voices or instruments an impossibility.'[18] The only evidence of a serialist approach in *The Turn of the Screw* is confined to the method of creating transformations of the theme. In the orchestral interludes at least, the theme is not 'developed' in a Classical/Romantic sense; rather it is manipulated by means of neo-Baroque devices of inversion and retrograde movement, augmentation and diminution, devices adopted by serialist composers in the twentieth century. That these treatments are already implicit in the theme itself will become apparent if we compare the intervallic relationships between the three cells of the theme.

Although the sense of traditional tonality arises most strongly from the melodic lines, it is underpinned by a texture which is predominantly harmonic rather than contrapuntal, with chords based on segments of the theme sounded simultaneously (another serial technique). This treatment, too, is foreshadowed in the original statement of the theme, and can be seen in the cumulative harmonies produced as each new note is added and sustained. Chords derived in this way will tend to be based on superimposed fourths rather than traditional triads (see Variation II, below, p. 77), and generate a blunt-edged and mildly dissonant harmonic vocabulary, at times clearly based on the whole-tone scale and always sounding very different from the sensuous, neo-Renaissance consonances of *Gloriana* (1953); triads, however, are not avoided (for example in Variation III, below, p. 78), and the theme also yields sequences of seventh chords (using notes 1-2-3, 5-6-7, or 2-3-4, 6-7-8 etc.) which influence both melody and harmony at the most tender moments in the drama (notably the governess's letter-writing in Act II scene 3). A sense of tonality is so firmly established in the opera that Britten could exploit it to create bitonal clashes for dramatic purposes (as in Act II scene 8, see below, pp. 100-1) – a technique he had explored in some detail in *Billy Budd* (1951). And this varied harmonic vocabulary is fastidiously scored throughout to involve timbre as the equal of pitch: once again the technique is implicit in the original statement of the theme, which assigns each of the twelve notes its individual colour. Erwin Stein felt that the Screw theme generated, by its melodic and harmonic implications, so strong an influence over the entire musical language of the opera that it created a new and individual musical style, unique to this opera, which he called 'the idiom of the piece'![9]

Both the variation interludes and the opera scenes grow out of the Screw theme but they use it differently. The variation interludes make the clearer contact with the theme, some indeed being decorative variations in the strictest sense, with the theme always present and always easily heard. Variation II is of this kind. This interlude concludes Act I scene 2, *The Welcome*. It derives from that scene a rhythmic texture which contrasts the sustained minims of the governess's music –

Ex. 10

- with a scampering quaver movement in compound time which is associated with the children:

Ex. 11

A specific representational significance is given to Variation II when Mrs Grose sings, to the same metre as the children's music, 'In a trice they'll be dragging you all over the park'. The interlude, then, depicts this 'guided tour' and also represents the short interval of time (two days in James, unspecified in the opera) of untroubled living at Bly between the governess's arrival and Act I scene 3, *The Letter.*

Variation II is intimately related to the preceding scene. The final ensemble of Act I scene 2 has the governess's sustained phrases floating above the busy texture and slightly lower tessitura assigned to Mrs Grose and the children. In the variation, the even minims from her confident phrase 'How charming. . .they are' are transferred to the bass of the variation and the Screw theme, transposed to C (more about the transpositions of the theme in the variations on p. 93 below), is enunciated in this even metre below the children's music. It is a simple but graphic portrayal of the children seen through the governess's eyes, and the steady pace of the minims suggests her serene and self-controlled bearing, her initial forebodings quieted, at this early stage of the opera.

The Screw theme in the bass is built up gradually (see Ex. 12). We shall find this cumulative treatment of the theme recurring in the opera. The full statement of the theme is followed by its inversion, after which it is gradually dismantled in much the same manner as it was built up, finishing on a pedal C which binds this variation to the following scene. Above this bass the children's music is thickened out with chords derived from the theme itself. Of course when the theme is a twelve-note one, any chord can be shown to be derived from it, but the high proportion of chords throughout the opera which are formed from a superimposition of the first three or four notes of the theme (and each cell of the 'row' yields the same intervals) is evidence of the source of Britten's harmonic vocabulary in this work. The chords which appear in, for example, bar 3 of the original statement of the theme (see above, p. 73) and in bars 6–8 of Variation II are strongly characteristic of the 'idiom of the piece'.

Variation II shows Britten's most mechanical manipulation of the Screw theme. By contrast, Variation III (very much of a second thought – see above, p. 67) presents a freer use of the note row. Both the serial application and the effect are more relaxed. Moreover it is a melodic variation. The theme appears in the upper parts only, over a static bass. This tone poem, evoking a summer evening, forms a deceptively soothing prologue to Act I scene 4, *The Tower.* Britten spins serene woodwind melismata out of segments of the theme (see

Ex. 12

Variation II The lights fade as the children lead the Governess off.
With movement ($\d$ =76)
GOVERNESS

Ex. 13). He does not hesitate to change the order of notes within each cell when the melodic line is better served, and the strongly stated D major tonality is less threatened, by the inversion (see Ex. 14). The mood darkens when the clarinet replaces oboe and flute, and the simple tonics and dominants of D major are displaced by a swirling A♭ arpeggio over a sustained chord of F major. But the most striking musical event in this variation is the sounding of the last note of the theme (F) by a high, staccato bassoon. It is an

Ex. 13

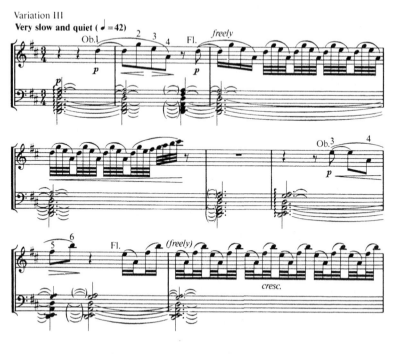

Ex. 14

unscheduled entry: the theme has been introduced cumulatively, with only one inversion of the expected note order (quoted above). The ninth and tenth notes of the theme, the falling Bb–Eb which mark the climax of the clarinet arpeggios, have dominated the five bars which precede the bassoon entry, and there has been no hint of a melodically prominent C, the eleventh note of the row, even though it could have been accommodated either in the context of the F major harmony or the Ab major melody (see Ex. 15). These

Ex. 15

remarkable bars well illustrate the layers of significance the rich idiom of this opera can sustain, and the integration of musical and dramatic effects. In terms of the variation technique used throughout the opera, the bassoon F completes the theme (albeit by leaping over the missing C which is briefly passed through in the final arpeggio of the movement). On a representational level, the entry introduces a remarkably realistic bird-call into the nocturnal tone poem. In terms of the drama, it gives added significance to a passage which occurs in the next scene, Act I scene 4. Here, above the same dry bassoon figure (on A and C♯), the governess sings,

Only one thing I wish, that I could see him –
and that he could see how well I do his bidding

and shortly afterwards she sees a figure on the tower which she believes to be the guardian. In this scene, the bassoon solo becomes associated with the fatal brooding on an unrequited passion to which adherents of the 'second story' attribute the governess's eventual insanity. And in the collaboration between the musical technique of Variation III and the psychological revelations of Act I scene 4, it is possible to read these bars as both a literal and a metaphorical *leaping to (false) conclusions*: the Screw theme leaps to its final note, the governess agitatedly misconstrues the appearance of Quint on the tower ("Tis he!'). A fanciful interpretation perhaps, but the very least we can say about this passage is that Britten has exploited the expectations aroused by the serial process prevalent throughout the opera to create a notable point of tension whose dramatic significance we can only grasp when we hear the passage repeated in the following scene. What is prepared for in Variation III is not the appearance of Quint on the tower but the governess's state of mind, in which the longed-for presence of the guardian is very nearly successfully conjured up.

A brief look at one more variation will serve to indicate the range of treatments of the Screw theme in the interludes. The serial treatment this time is vertical and derives from bar 9 of the original statement of the theme. Variation XV precedes the final scene of the opera. Everything in it speaks of cumulation, of opposition of extremes and of the imminent confrontation of those extremes which will take place in Act II scene 8, *Miles*. The variation, only five bars long, has five distinct events. A huge chord, which superimposes all the notes of the theme, swells from *ppp* to *fff* and explodes in a cadenza for solo piccolo which falls through two octaves in the halting rhythm associated with Flora's denunciation of the governess in the previous scene:

I can't see anybody, can't see anything, nobody, nothing, nobody, nothing; I don't know what you mean.   (II. 7)

A second chord, also conflating the theme though at different registers and differently scored, swells and is released by a cadenza for timpani, loosely inverting the piccolo passage. The final throw of this variation is a third statement of the Screw chord which again crescendos and stammers out two more, briefer crescendi before finally subsiding as the scene opens in a heavy reminiscence in the bass of Mrs Grose's memorable exclamation, 'Dear God, is there no end to his dreadful ways?' (I. 5). This variation opposes, in the two cadenzas, whatever was innocent at Bly with whatever was malign. Crushed between the disorienting dissonances of the Screw chords, the real pathos of the piccolo solo faces the unequivocal threat of the timpani line, and the verbal associations which saturate the 'Dear God' theme offer no comfortable solution.

The variation interludes, then, provide a framework for the opera – both for the unfolding of the story and the structural processes of the instrumental music. They advance, through a series of literal variations on the Screw theme, a musical counterpart of the mounting terror at Bly.[20] But they do not provide the only context in which the Screw theme is heard. It invades the scenes of the opera too, and, with one exception (see below, p. 90), every character in the story expresses their most urgent feelings in notes which derive from the Screw theme. This gives the theme an enhanced status in the drama. It draws connexions between the governess and Quint and Quint and the children. And its omnipresence mirrors the governess's obsession with the malign infection which she diagnoses in – or spreads throughout – the household at Bly.

To call the opera scenes a second set of variations on the Screw theme would be an exaggeration. Their musical function, like their dramatic purpose, differs from the interludes, and not every scene displays the theme as continuously as all the variations do (though some scenes, for example Act II scene 4, *The Bedroom*, derive almost every bar from some aspect of the theme). The Screw theme does, however, influence the shape of the majority of the melodies which appear in the scenes, and it continues to generate much of the harmony. Erwin Stein's perception of its all-pervasive influence on the stylistic idiom of the opera can be confirmed as readily from the scenes as from the interludes.

The Screw theme appears intact in three of the scenes. It frames each act. Having opened the opera proper, it sounds in the orchestra at the climax of Act I scene 8 (fig. 87 in the score), it is sung by the ghosts in Act II scene 1, and appears both in the bass and sung by the governess at the climax of Act II scene 8 (fig. 131). Apart from these reappearances, there are three principal derivations from it, one associated with the governess, Quint and Mrs Grose, another used by Quint, the governess and both children, and a third assigned exclusively (and less satisfactorily because of this) to Miss Jessel. The technique of associating specific themes with certain characters is not to be confused with the process of *Leitmotiv* as Britten had operated it, for example, in *The Rape of Lucretia* (a rather mechanical process which often appears irritatingly naïve) and the more subtle use in *Billy Budd*. In *The Turn of the Screw* the technique is used not to identify and individualise characters but to draw connexions between them, and to imply relationships which could not be articulated verbally without losing the intrinsic ambiguity of the story. That is to say, there *is* a 'governess motif' *and* a 'Quint motif', but as a consequence of the underlying variation form of the whole opera, these motifs can be shown to be variations of each other, both deriving from the central Screw theme. The dramatic bonus is that Quint and the governess express their relationship with the children in analogous (and sometimes nearly identical) material – so that the technique becomes a further example of the fusion of musical structure and the demands of this very demanding drama.

Arnold Whittall has drawn attention to Britten's increasingly subtle use of unifying devices, already discernible in *Peter Grimes*:

> Britten's fluency as a music-dramatist depended on the flexible application of a very simple formal principle, or scale of procedures, in which the successive stages of the action are unified and related by exact or varied recurrences of material. Indeed, his development as an opera composer may best be described in terms of the testing and elaboration of some more far-reaching unifying principle for each work than is provided by recurring motives alone.   (Whittall, *The Music of Britten and Tippett*, pp. 97–8)

Certainly the creation and manipulation of motifs in *The Turn of the Screw* is worked out on an entirely new level of structural ingenuity and dramatic significance and, moreover, a good proportion of both the technical means and the dramatic ends are able to be perceived by the first-time listener who has not studied the score – a point which would have had high priority with Britten.

The first derivation can be called the 'catalyst' theme because it is continuously associated with the governess's coming to Bly and the impact this has on the events of the story. It first occurs in Act I scene 1 at a significant point in the governess's musings (see Ex. 16).

Ex. 16

This theme is intrinsically expressive of self-doubt and indecision, with its fluid rhythm allowing a reflective pause on the first 'why' and a hint of the governess's fatal impetuosity in the accelerated downward plunge on the second (*facilis descensus averni*); the tortuous shape of the theme, with its apposition of F♯ and F♮, E♮ and E♭, is similarly highly expressive of the governess's nervous vulnerability. (These incipient false relations are most strongly developed in the governess's letter music in Act II scene 3 – a scene which marks the climax of the governess's characterisation as a vulnerable innocent, after which, as she hardens into a more heroic – or more insane – certainty, the chromatic inflexions are gradually removed from her music.)

The catalyst theme appears frequently in the early scenes to indicate an underlying uneasiness. In Act I scene 2, *The Welcome*, it ironically accompanies the governess's assertion,

You must be Mrs Grose? I'm so happy to see you. . .
so happy to be here.   (I. 2 fig. 9)

and Mrs Grose takes up the first motif – the descending fourth with its upward turn of a tone – to echo these words:

I'm so happy, so happy that you've come, Miss.   (I. 2 fig. 10)

A longer reminiscence of the theme hangs evilly in the air during the governess's revelation in Act I scene 3 of Miles's dismissal from school. And a tingling statement in parallel major sevenths on oboe and horn accompanies the governess's discovery that Quint is dead and her realisation that she has seen a ghost:

Is this sheltered place
the wicked world where things unspoken of can be?   (I. 5 fig. 44)

Towards the end of Act I the governess expands the theme into a despairing outburst, which depicts her scarcely-suppressed hysteria in a nervous sequential repetition of the final motif:

I neither save nor shield them,
I keep nothing from them.
Oh I am useless, useless.   (I. 7 fig. 69)

In the second act, the meaning assigned to the catalyst theme darkens as the objective presence of evil begins to close in. The theme is specifically attached to the idea of loss of innocence when the ghosts revive its original form to sing:

The ceremony of innocence is drowned.   (II. 1)

The governess takes up the opening motif, once used to express Mrs Grose's 'So happy that you've come' (I. 2), to speak her self-doubts:

That his house is poisoned, the children mad – or that I am! (II. 2 fig. 38)

And it is surely no coincidence that the governess expresses her sense of being trapped at Bly with the same notes in which she first questioned her wisdom in coming:

I can't go, I can't, I can't.   (II. 3 fig. 64)

Her relationship with Flora is focused on the parallel scenes Act I scene 7 and Act II scene 7. At the conclusion of Act I scene 7 she used the catalyst theme to voice her failure to shield the children. At the equivalent point in Act II scene 7, she confesses in related phrases to a more radical failure:

I have failed, most miserably failed, and there is no more innocence in me
(II. 7 fig. 113)

But the very same theme can be manipulated to express confidence – regardless of the fact that that confidence is as groundless as the earlier unease. At the conclusion of Act II scene 6, the governess is at a high point of certainty. She is convinced that she has evidence of Miles's corruption – that he has colluded with Flora to provide a diversion, enabling her to escape to be with Miss Jessel. In a new version of the catalyst theme, she sings

Ex. 17

GOVERNESS

Oh, I___don't mind that now, ___ he's   with Quint!

The bold rising fourth ('that now'), replacing the major second, makes this phrase a direct quotation from Quint's seductive call in Act I scene 8 (see below) and is a further example of the confusion of identity between Quint and the governess which we noticed in Chapter 2: not only does she appear at 'his' window and on 'his' tower, but she shares the motif with which she believes he lures Miles to destruction.

This new version of the catalyst theme colours her intermittent but increasing moments of confidence in the last scenes of the opera. For example when we hear the identical notes sung by Flora in Act II scene 7 we know that we are hearing her through the governess's ears (see Ex. 18). Flora's childish outburst sounds to the governess like a parody of Quint's supernatural summons, and confirms her in her persuasion that Flora is irredeemably corrupted.

The most telling use of this variant, however, is in Act II scene 8,

Ex. 18

FLORA

I can't see a - ny - bo - dy, can't see a - ny-thing

where she claims Miles in a passionate outburst (the culmination of her confusion of identity with Quint); the rhythmic waywardness and the chromatic twists of the original catalyst theme are banished with her doubts (see Ex. 19).

Ex. 19

Slow and regular (♩ =60)

GOVERNESS *passionately*

O Miles____ I can-not bear to__ lose you. You shall be___

Timp. Db. (pizz.) Harp.

mine, and I shall save you.__

Variants of the catalyst theme are associated with two other characters, Quint and Mrs Grose. Quint's version is an elaborate embellishment, totally chilling, yet a temptation (see Ex. 20). Mrs Grose's version is her magnificently simple reaction to evidence of

Ex. 20

QUINT *freely*

Miles! _____

Miles!_____

Ex. 21

Quint's presence (see Ex. 21). It has the outlines of a heartfelt sigh. We feel she has used this phrase a dozen times in Quint's lifetime, and that for her the horror of his haunting is less immediate than her exasperation at the revival of a trouble she had thought to be rid of.

The connexion between these themes and the Screw theme can now be shown (see Ex. 22). What this somewhat dry and analytical

Ex. 22

chart does not show is the ease with which these 'family resemblances' are perceived by the untaught listener, and the tantalising scope for varied interpretation they present. In Act I scene 4, *The Tower*, for example, the governess, musing on her desire to see her employer again, sings (over the bassoon figure already discussed; see above, p. 79)

Only one thing I wish, that I could see him –
and that he could see how well I do his bidding.

The words 'his bidding' are then repeated to a quotation from the catalyst theme (see Ex. 23).

Ex. 23

This passage seems to me to stem from the first 'Why, why did I come?' – answering the initial question with the response 'to do his bidding'. Anthony Besch, however (see Chapter 4, p. 143), hears this as a premonition of Quint's presence – a quotation from Quint's version of the catalyst theme– and thus a clue to the confusion in the governess's mind between the guardian and the ghost, a confusion which is to be manifested in the immediately ensuing bars when the figure appears on the tower. There is, of course, no uniquely right interpretation of these bars: only an infinite richness of resonance and association.

The second major derivation from the Screw theme is a brief three-note motif initially associated with Quint, though it invades the governess's music and that of the children, establishing a relationship between the four of them. The first appearance of the motif (see Ex. 24) is ambiguous. A first-time audience can only register it as

Ex. 24

a mere introductory flourish to the catalyst theme – but a disturbing one. The distinctive tone colour of the celesta is arresting. The audience is put in the same position as the governess – we feel something must be radically wrong but we don't know what.

This little motif – it appears both melodically and as a chord, and is clearly formed from the third, second and fourth notes of the

Screw theme on A♭ – is soon associated directly with Quint. It is
heard when Quint appears on the tower (I. 4 fig. 26), and at the window (I. 5 fig. 35) and is present almost throughout Act I scene 8. A
more subtle touch is that it is heard whenever anyone on stage is
thinking about Quint. The bells chime it insistently at fig. 38 of
Act II scene 2 when the governess betrays her thoughts by singing of
the 'poisoned' house. In Act II scene 4, Miles is 'sitting and thinking'
in his bedroom. 'Of what are you thinking?' asks the governess, and
we need not be deceived by Miles's evasive answer, for the harp
whispers the Quint chord throughout every line the boy sings. (This
accompaniment is silent during the governess's questions.) Britten
preserves James's ambiguities by allowing the harp to represent
either Miles's thoughts of Quint or the thoughts the governess
imputes to him.

The governess herself uses a variant of the Quint motif (a simple
re-ordering of the notes) when she first sees the unknown figure on
the tower (see Ex. 25).

Ex. 25

Who is it?   Who?

The words express the question, the notes answer it. This motif
returns repeatedly in the opera. In Act I it represents a genuine question in her mind: for example the extended portrayal of panic in
Act I scene 5 when the governess sees Quint at the window, the similar passage when she first sees Miss Jessel in Act I scene 7, and when
she discovers the children up at night in Act I scene 8. In Act II she is
confident that she knows the agent of corruption, and the motif
reappears whenever she attempts to make Miles name Quint: her
temporising questions – 'Why, Miles, not yet in bed? Not even
undressed?' (II. 4 fig. 71), 'Miles, dear little Miles, is there nothing
you want to tell me?' (II. 4 fig. 75) – are set to the Quint motif, and
the notes reveal what she is really asking about. In the last scene of
the second act, words and music coincide as she presses Miles to
answer the question which has dominated her life at Bly: 'Is who
there, Miles? Say it!' (II. 8 fig. 130).

Most disturbingly, the Quint motif can be shown to have per-
meated to the hearts of the children. It shapes their most equivocal
expressions:

Ex. 26

Finally Miss Jessel: that Miss Jessel is somewhat unsatisfactorily drawn in the opera is in part due to James. James's governess, and therefore Britten's, is simply less interested in her predecessor than in the male triangle of the guardian, Miles and Quint. Moreover, Flora's role is deliberately muted in the opera; Britten was perhaps wary of weakening the impersonation of a child by an adult singer (see Chapter 4) by over-exposing her voice or tempting her into betraying a mature acting ability. Miss Jessel's eclipse is the result of both these tendencies – both the governess's involvement with the male characters and Flora's subservience to Miles. (However, Mrs Grose is similarly placed but has nevertheless a strong musical personality.) At least a partial cause of Miss Jessel's ill-defined role must be the nature of the music assigned to her. It is – given the tight structuring of the opera it would be unthinkable were it otherwise – based on a further derivation from the Screw theme. But, in contrast to the catalyst theme and the Quint motif, the derivation is not easy to hear, and this fact detaches her from the centre of the drama.

To trace her Screw-oriented musical characterisation it is necessary to return to the theme. In its skeleton form beginning on F♯ it can be seen to be formed from two interlocking whole-tone scales, the sequences identified as 1a–6a and 1b–6b in Ex. 27. Miss Jessel's

Ex. 27

characterising motif is based on the lower scale. This arpeggiated chord accompanies most of Miss Jessel's appearances (for example I. 8 fig. 79, II. 1 fig. 18, II. 7 fig. 104). Like the Quint motif, it is also heard in those contexts where the ghost is present only in the governess's thoughts:

Flora's gone, gone out to her. . .
Come, we must go and find her!   (II. 6)

The whole-tone scale occasionally colours Miss Jessel's melodic line – for example her bird-like invocation of Flora in fig. 79 of Act I scene 8. But the basic motif is neither memorable in itself nor easily perceived to be derived from the Screw theme. Furthermore, there is the unaccountable fact that whenever the governess, Quint and Mrs Grose are driven to extremes of emotion, and Miles and Flora articulate their most disturbingly ambiguous thoughts, their music becomes ever more closely bound to the Screw-derived motifs we have traced in the preceding pages. But with Miss Jessel the reverse happens. Her most intense utterances, notably her lament in the schoolroom scene in Act II scene 3, appear to have little audible connexion with her allotted motif. Her character lacks musical consistency and in consequence we find her less interesting.

III The climax: Act II scene 8, *Miles*

PATRICIA HOWARD

The musical structure of *The Turn of the Screw* is innately intricate. Erwin Stein wrote:

The idiom of *The Turn of the Screw* is unmistakable, and its analysis gives us a fascinating look into the workshop of a composer's mind. Among the thematic and other connections here discussed are some of which the composer was not even aware as he wrote – he was rather surprised, when told, about the secrets hidden in his music.   (Stein, p. 6)

He was close enough to the composer, though, to be able to confirm that 'most of the combinations. . . have been worked out quite consciously'. Peter Evans has written of the same phenomenon from the listener's point of view: 'Much that analysis reveals may not have been consciously registered, yet all has been felt' (*The Music of Benjamin Britten*, p. 222). The density of the structural processes in this opera have made it necessary to review, however briefly, the interrelationships in the whole opera in order to understand the organisation of a single scene.

7 Original production, 1954, Act II scene 8. Peter Pears, David Hemmings,
Jennifer Vyvyan. Producer, Basil Coleman; designer, John Piper.

Act II scene 8 is in two senses the climax of the opera. Self-evidently it provides the dramatic climax, the culmination of the inevitable tragedy, set in motion by the governess's catalytic arrival at Bly. Her growing involvement with Miles, her need to question every area of his experience which falls outside her direct observation, her compulsion to dominate him, to isolate him from his guardian, from Flora, from Mrs Grose and from the possibility of Quint's lingering – or continuing – influence lead inevitably to the final scene. Here we find the final episode in the interrogation of the boy, which the governess has pursued relentlessly ever since the early schoolroom scenes represented by Act I scene 6. The scene also includes the long-anticipated duel with Quint. The governess has never seemed so confident, so much in control, so that even an adherent to the exclusive truth of the 'first story' must question what the concept of 'possession' really means and who, in this last scene, is 'possessed'. Musically the scene is a climax too, and for the same reason: it is a culmination. The drama has been worked out in two separate, interleaved musical structures, the interludes and the scenes. Act II scene 8 brings these two structures to a common resolution. It unifies the diverse variational techniques displayed in the two parallel sequences of movements and completes both the inaudible order and the audible. In a quite special, technical sense, it is *both the final variation and the final scene.*

First, the inaudible order. An aspect of the overall form not yet considered is the tonal scheme of the opera. There are two basic approaches to musical analysis: that which tries to reconstruct the composer's thought-processes, and that which takes as its starting point what the listener hears. All the thematic connexions we have so far noted, with the exception of Miss Jessel's motif, have been easy to hear. Any discussion of large-scale tonal organisation, however, falls uncompromisingly within the first approach. And in view of the fact that this type of musical structuring is unrecognisable (though its effects are not necessarily unperceivable) by more than ninety per cent of any normal opera-going audience, its relevance in a book offered principally to the music lover rather than to the professional student is open to question. However, tonal organisation is a matter of very great moment to all composers. Britten may have been unaware of all the thematic connexions generated by his Screw theme but his tonal plan could not have come about by chance. It is a paradox that the thematic connexions are easy to detect but may have been created largely unconsciously, while the tonal relationships, which are difficult for an audience which has not studied the score to trace, were undoubtedly consciously devised and employed.

The tonal scheme of this opera is irresistible in its logic.[21] The scheme embraces both scenes and variations. We have noticed in passing that the Screw theme is transposed for each variation and that each scene is oriented substantially in the same key area as the preceding variation. The cycle of keys throughout the opera can be seen in Ex. 28. The key centre of Variation XII is obscure. Eric

Ex. 28

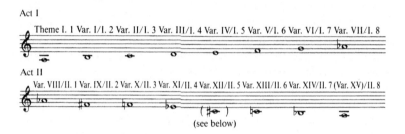

(see below)

Walter White (*Benjamin Britten: his Life and Operas*, p. 182) identified it as E major, and certainly this key is more strongly felt in the companion scene, Act II scene 5. There is, however, sufficient ambiguity in Variation XII for us to assign the expected tonality of C♯ (minor) at least to the opening bars. And 'expected' is the clue. The sequence of tonal centres forms an orderly progression not merely (as Erwin Stein suggested, p. 7) up the 'white note' keys and down predominantly 'black' ones, but, as Peter Evans has pointed out (*The Music of Benjamin Britten*, p. 206), the Act II key sequence is an exact inversion of the tone and semitone steps of Act I.

In terms of this scheme the opera has to end in A. The semitone step which placed Variation VII and Act I scene 8 in the key of A♭ (a key hardly touched on elsewhere in Act I and reserved significantly for the motif denoting Quint's presence and the songs suggesting his sphere of influence – 'Malo' and 'On the paths, in the woods') should shift Variation XV and Act II scene 8 just as inevitably from B♭ to A. But this final, expected key is resisted. Variation XV, briefly described above (p. 80), is tonally indeterminate (though it subsides on a strongly suggestive dominant E in bar 4 of Act II scene 8) and the secure A major in which the passacaglia opens is fiercely contested when Quint appears and recapitulates his A♭ music from Act I scene 8. The dramatic duel between the governess and Quint is thus played out on another level between the keys of A and Ab. This tonal battle is easily recognised as it takes place by the audience, but only those listeners who have been able to follow the overall key scheme of the opera are in a position to know that the A tonality, associated here with the governess, must overcome the Ab Quint tonality for the opera to reach its calculated conclusion. The irony of the tonal drama lies in the fact that the triumph of A over Ab (which is implicit from the moment the passacaglia starts: it is not in the nature of passacaglias to end in a different key from the one they started in) is no victory at all for the governess.

The idea of opposing key centres generating a dramatic conflict is of course traditional in European music of the last three hundred years, and indeed the raison d'être of all Classical forms. Britten, however, has here used it to create an analogue of the drama taking place on stage, and one whose far-reaching ramifications are even now still being scrutinised. Arnold Whittall, for example, suggests that the key scheme implies a dramatic resolution which does not in fact take place: 'Logically. . . it might be argued that the retreat in Act II from the supernatural evils of Ab to the starting point A, albeit by another route from that traversed in Act I, is more appropriate for a subject which ends, if not with a positive resolution, then at least with a restoration of the status quo' (*The Music of Britten and Tippett*, p. 161). He compares the ending of *The Turn of the Screw* with that of *Billy Budd* which has a conflict similarly expressed in keys a semitone apart, and finds in the earlier opera 'the ultimate "victory" of Bb [over B♮]. . . distinctly hollow, if not utterly sham'. He concedes, however, that 'the structural scheme of *The Turn of the Screw* seems right because of its rigour and coherence'. As Arnold Whittall perceived, there are limits to the burden of symbolism which we can load onto the essentially autonomous discipline of tonality. Structures in tonal music (unlike those in literature, though comparable with those in architecture) have to satisfy criteria other than dramatic truth and it is perhaps in consequence of his understanding of this point that Britten 'followed most opera composers in using thematic material, rather than tonality, to carry the principal weight of extra-musical association' (Whittall, *The Music of Britten and Tippett*, p. 161).

The audible order of Act II scene 8 provides many points of reference for those unable to follow the tonal drama. The scene falls into three units. It opens with a passage of recitative, punctuated with

three reminiscences of Mrs Grose's heavy phrase, 'Dear God. . . '.
These quotations (in the orchestra) are invested with a literal and
ominous eloquence as they imply 'no end' to Quint's 'dreadful ways'
– not that Quint is mentioned in this part of the scene, which aims to
establish both women's complete conviction of the children's
depravity. That it is *Quint's* 'dreadful ways' which are blamed for
Flora's corruption is a further diminution of Miss Jessel's role – a
diminution which does not originate with the opera. In James, Mrs
Grose seems to associate Flora's 'appalling language' with Quint,
though the point is not unambiguous.[22] In the opera, Quint's musical character is so much more fully defined than Miss Jessel's that
very specific meanings can be conjured up by brief musical references, so that when Mrs Grose begins, 'Such a night as I have spent –',
the phrase 'Dear God. . .' on the harp interrupts her, and attributes
the 'horrors' of Flora's outpourings to their proper source. The economy with which non-verbal reference is made in this exchange
exactly parallels the unspoken suggestions in James's scene.

Quint's corrupting influence is now shown to be at work in Miles:
when Mrs Grose reveals that the governess's letter to the guardian
has disappeared, the harp again voices their thoughts before either
speaks (see Ex. 29). The recitative section ends with a rising phrase,
expressing *melodically* the confidence which the purposeful move
towards A major implies *tonally*: 'All the same, go, and I shall stay
and face what I have to face with the boy.' This rising scale flows into
the opening of the passacaglia as the governess sings the last 'turn' of
the catalyst theme over the Screw theme in the bass. (This passage is
quoted above, p. 85.)

To build an active dramatic climax on a passacaglia structure was
something new for Britten. To be sure, passacaglias, chaconnes and
all types of variation form are found throughout his music from the
earliest years.[23] But his previous use of this process in opera had been
exclusively in static, meditative contexts, where the dramatic situation is summed up rather than developed: the Fourth Interlude in
Peter Grimes expresses a poignant causality between the doomed
apprentice and Grimes's fate; in *The Rape of Lucretia*, among a variety of ground bass treatments, the funeral march 'This dead hand
lets fall' is designed to be a formalised, non-realistic account of the
varied reactions to Lucretia's death; *Albert Herring*, composed to be
a companion piece to *Lucretia* and parodying it on every level, does
not omit to mock the tragic passacaglia in the threnody, 'In the midst
of life is death'; and even *The Little Sweep* (in its way a companion

Ex. 29

piece to *Grimes*) employs a miniature passacaglia to underline the
irony in 'Help, help! She's collapsed'. These passacaglias all exploit
their form to bind together the diverse emotional reactions to a
single situation. An unnatural intensity is created, whether for tragic
or comic effect.

   The Turn of the Screw uses the genre quite differently. Act II scene
8 is a highly dramatic scene, full of incident and changing situations. The difference lies partly in the theme itself: by this stage in the
opera the Screw theme is very familiar indeed and portentous with
verbal and musical significance. It is used to create a strong sense of
inevitability, of a crisis, long avoided, which will not this time be
side-stepped.

   Britten had already foreshadowed his treatment of the bass here in
several earlier variations. The cumulative statement of the theme we
noted in Variation II and Variation III is established in the first six
variations as a convention, as an aspect of the 'idiom' of the opera.
Variation IV builds up the theme in the bass in a process not
unrelated to Variation II; Variation V is a series of quasi-fugal

entries, each one displaying two notes of the theme as the music modulates through a circle of keys; Variation VI is not unrelated to Variation III in its employment of arpeggios (in the bass this time), each of which culminates in a new pair of notes being added to the theme (again, the procedure produces wide-ranging modulations). Later variations treat the Screw theme both more strictly (Variations VII and X) and more freely (Variations VIII and XII), but the cumulative technique has been established and held, as it were, in reserve for the moment in the drama when a sense of anticipation, of movement towards fulfilment, is most needed.

The progress of the drama towards its climax is measured by the completion of the bass. The first stage takes place over the first six notes of the theme (see p. 85). These are enunciated eight times. The music remains rooted on A, sometimes major, sometimes minor. The words suggest the reticent exchanges of James's 'young couple . . . on their wedding journey'.[24] Each phrase is full of dangerous resonances which are damped by lack of response in the other:

Miles: So, my dear, we are alone.
Governess: Are we alone?
Miles: O, I'm afraid so.
Governess: Do you mind? do you mind being left alone?
Miles: Do you?

The returns of the foreshortened passacaglia bass convey the frustrations of this dialogue. But the mood affects the characters differently, for while the governess's melodic line blossoms into scarcely-concealed declarations of love (see Ex. 30), Miles feels trapped, and

Ex. 30

Dear-est Miles, I love ____ to be with you ____ What else should I stay for?

his music is a series of variants on his constricted opening phrase (Ex. 31).

Ex. 31

So, my dear, we are a - lone

During the eight statements of notes 1–6 of the bass the music has stayed obstinately on A and the action on stage has stagnated. The second phase of the finale begins when the governess asks, 'What it is. . . you have on your mind'. (We are reminded of Act II scene 4 where the governess probed Miles's thoughts and brought upon herself evidence of Quint's presence acting as an inhibition on Miles.) As if in direct answer to her question, the bass begins its cycle of eight notes and the plot moves forward again as the voice of Quint enters with his seductive variant of the catalyst theme. The way in which this entry takes place over a 'leap' in the bass from note 2 to note 4 recalls the 'leaping to conclusions' in Variation III; the movement of the bass also secures maximum dissonance at Quint's entry, and a hint of the bitonal drama to come (see Ex. 32).

Ex. 32

There are four repetitions of notes 1–8. The interrogation seems to be getting stuck again. Miles is on the verge of responding but Quint's intervention silences him:

Miles: I will tell you everything. I will!
Quint: No!
Miles: But not now.

Over the final statement of the eight-note phase of the theme, the governess asks Miles, 'Did you steal my letter?' and the eighth note, G♯ (= A♭), is prolonged while Quint appears on the tower (but see Chapter 2, p. 60), the more effectively to silence Miles – or to fulfil the governess's imaginings. Miles, however, admits his theft and the music is wrenched triumphantly back to A major as the governess consolidates her victory over a reprise of notes 1–4:

Governess: Why did you take it?
Miles: To see what you said about us.
Quint: Be silent!

The next section of the passacaglia brings rapid advances to the drama. Over a statement of nine notes of the theme, the governess continues to press Miles ('Who is it you see? Who do you wait for, watch for?') with a variant of her 'Who is it?' phrase (p. 36), shorn of its nervous, snatching rhythm, since the governess is now confident she knows the answer. The ninth note of the theme is prolonged as Quint makes another appeal ('Do not betray our secrets! Beware of her!') while Miles resorts once more to ambiguity – his 'I don't know what you mean' may be directed either at Quint or at the governess. The next statement reaches the tenth note, which is again prolonged as Quint sings in premature triumph, 'Miles, you are mine!' while Miles, ambiguous still, asks 'Is he there?' At this point in James, it will be remembered, Miles all but silenced the governess by asking 'Is she here? . . . Miss Jessel, Miss Jessel' (James, pp. 120–1). Britten and Piper had to sacrifice this tantalising confusion to maintain the now relentless pace of the unfolding climax. The full statement of the theme is reached at last as the governess and Quint make their rival demands on Miles, resulting in his shout of 'Nobody, nothing!' which recalls Flora's similar denial in Act II scene 7.

This is the point in the score (fig. 130–1) which was originally planned to be the climax of the scene, as Donald Mitchell has revealed in his valuable account of Britten's revisions ('Britten's Revisionary Practice', p. 18). In the first version, which Mitchell prints in this article, the last and only complete statement of the theme is a nervous striving version which stutters out the pattern

– a microcosm of the growth the Screw theme has undergone in the preceding passacaglia. Britten must have had a number of reasons for rejecting this version but among them may well have been the realisation that, for the final statement of the Screw theme in the opera, this urgent climax was neither aurally perceptible enough, to an audience who had not traced the progress of the passacaglia in the score, nor weighty enough to match the other complete statements of the theme which seem designed to frame the opera: the first statement (in A) which concludes the Prologue, the horn statement (in Ab) in Act I scene 8 and the sung version in Ab in Act II scene 1. The palindromic pattern of these conspicuous complete statements of the theme seems to demand a final statement (and in A) near the conclusion of the opera.

Britten's revised version has just that. From fig. 131, the complete theme is enunciated in the bass in its original rhythm with the fourth, eighth and twelfth notes prolonged as in the initial appearance (p. 73). Above this, the governess sings a closely-related melodic line which continues to bombard Miles with questions, while Quint returns to his song from Act I scene 7, 'On the paths, in the woods', which maintains a detached Ab major against the bass and governess's music, which are in A. Miles is silent. The 'tonal battle' of the opera climax, then, is extended and intensified in this version and is presented in a form which the audience can understand without a sense of absolute pitch. The themes are familiar, and they are presented over a long enough timespan (in comparison with the earlier version) for the audience not only to recognise but to experience through the bitonality the utterly irreconcilable pressures on Miles. His last scream of 'Peter Quint, you devil!' brings the passacaglia to its catastrophic close.

The final unit of the scene matches James's final, poignant paragraph. It uses the audience's familiarity with the musical materials of the opera to point up a series of ambiguities: the right words in the wrong key, the right tune sung by the wrong singer. The confusions of identity between Quint, the governess and Miles, which the unique structure of the opera was designed to display, are manifest in this scene when, for the first time in the opera, the governess sings in unison with Quint, and finally takes up Miles's 'Malo' song.

At the end of the passacaglia the conflicting sounds of A and A♭ hang unresolved in the air, though it is over an A pedal that Miles shouts his last ambiguous words. The pedal A implies victory for the governess, but immediately the last section of the scene begins with a plunge into A♭, and a texture of 'Quint chords' (see above, p. 87) accompany Quint and the governess who sing, in octaves,

Governess: Ah Miles! you are saved!
Quint: Ah Miles! we have failed!

The words are, of course, a reversal of the truth; it is the unprecedented unison and the sustained 'Quint harmony' that betray reality. The governess's misapprehension strengthens as the music turns towards A, and, with almost unbearable unconscious irony she sings, 'Together we have destroyed him'. As if in confirmation of her triumph, Quint sings his last 'Farewell' to his own version of the catalyst theme but in E minor, the first time he has sung it in a 'sharp' key.

The last pages are dominated by the 'Malo' song, which begins on the cor anglais as the governess realises that the boy is dead. (We may recall the mourning music in *The Rape of Lucretia*, given to the same instrument, though enunciated before Lucretia's death.) At the climax of her emotion, she joins in the instrumental statement of the theme, bringing it to an uneasy cadence in Quint's key (G♯ = A♭) at fig. 138. The opera ends with a question. The governess's words make it an explicit one: 'What have we done between us?' But the 'Malo' theme, which she repeats in a low register, carries its own intrinsic puzzle which the opera has not solved. The last statement of 'Malo' is unfinished and the final bars bring the opera to an abrupt, whispered A major conclusion in the orchestra.[25]

IV The colour of the music

CHRISTOPHER PALMER

My brief in theory is to discuss Britten's orchestral technique as demonstrated in *The Turn of the Screw*; but I prefer the more general

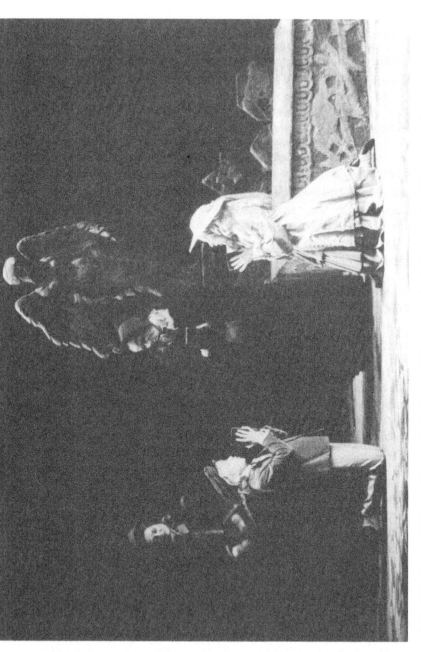

8 Scottish Opera, 1970, Act II scene 2. Catherine Wilson, Timothy Oldham, Judith Pierce, Nan Christie. Producer, Anthony Besch; designer, John Stoddart.

term 'colour' to orchestration, which – in Britten's case at least – surely belongs in James's category of 'weak specifications'. For in Britten 'orchestration' never exists in and for itself; it and the musical language to which it gives voice form an indivisible entity, the two components need to be examined the one in terms of another, and these in their turn can be fully understood only when we have formed the clearest possible picture of the forces that motivated the composer in his work – and they are complex. I make no apology for poaching on certain areas already partially covered by other contributors to this volume since I am attempting to complement, not duplicate, their efforts.

To begin at an important part of the beginning, namely the reasons which drew Britten to James in the first place: Vivien Jones notes that a prime concern of James's tale is the power of sexuality, a sensitive subject perhaps but one which has to bear further scrutiny if we are to recognise the true strength of relationship between author and composer. Homosexuality, incest, paedophilia, even nymphomania are all to some extent implied (never, of course, overtly stated) in James, but the central burden of interest is indubitably weighted on the first. What really drives the sexually repressed governess to distraction at Bly is the magnetic attraction of Miles to Quint; and in effect a horrifically un-conventional conventional triangular situation develops in which the governess, succumbing to Miles's seductiveness much as Miles had succumbed to Quint's, ends by frightening Miles to death[26] in preference to surrendering him to her rival. Now Britten, as is well known, was nearly always attracted to authors of a homosexual orientation – Auden, Rimbaud, Melville, Owen, Mann to name but a few – but so far no one has claimed this particular distinction for James, at least in relation to Britten. Yet the recurring theme of sexual repression in James – for example *Washington Square* and *The Aspern Papers* as well as *The Turn of the Screw* – argues a similar repression in James himself, amply documented by peers and contemporaries such as Wilde (who predicted in 1899 that James would 'never arrive at passion'), Somerset Maugham, who claimed that the characters in James's fiction 'have neither bowels nor sexual organs', and William Faulkner, who described James as 'the nicest old lady I know'. Yet towards the end of his life James emerged from the shadows to fall in love with not one but two beautiful young men half his age. From 1900 to 1913 he carried on a liaison with an American sculptor of Norwegian descent, and from 1903 to the end of his life adopted an

Irish boy of stunning good looks but apparently limited intelligence as a close companion, providing for him in his will. Then there is the literary evidence, not only of *The Turn of the Screw* but also – and fascinatingly from Britten's point of view – *The Pupil*, another short story with a disturbed young boy as its subject, first published in 1891. In it, Morgan Moreen, a precocious small boy with a weak heart, becomes inordinately attached to his young English tutor, and expires in a state of hyper-emotional excitement over his discredited parents' plan to place him permanently in the tutor's care. It is, in effect, a *Death-in-Venice*-type stuation in reverse; here it is the younger male, not the older, who is mortally ailing and susceptible. (Aschenbach, it will be remembered, dies on the beach of the 'sweet sea-city' of a heart attack induced by the prospect of his beloved Tadzio's leaving him.) The fact that part of the scene (though not the denouement) of *The Pupil* is actually set in Venice lends some incidental point to the analogy, as do the facts both that Venice was one of James's and Britten's favourite European cities, and that the latter's *The Turn of the Screw* was first performed there.

So much by way of preamble, and the reader is no doubt wondering at its specifically musical, as opposed to general documentary, relevance. The point is that since the Miles–Quint relationship lies at the deepest nerve-centre of both story and music – since the idea of the corruption of children (particularly that of a boy by an older man) fascinated both James and Britten as much as it appalled them – it makes good sense to examine in the first instance the music of Miles-and-Quint, since the likelihood is that it will have far-reaching consequences for the rest of the score. It does indeed. It is scarcely an exaggeration to describe Quint's very first manifestation-in-music – the tiny celesta flourish[27] (indicated by *x* in Ex. 33) when he appears to the governess on the tower – as a microcosm of the whole score in terms of (a) its timbre and (b) its constituent notes.

Thanks to the researches of Donald Mitchell we are now able to identify the provenance of the actual sound, the colour, of Quint's music. It is, of course, the gamelan or Balinese percussion orchestra. It is well known that Britten's exotic ballet *The Prince of the Pagodas* (1957) was a kind of musical report on his visit to Bali in 1956, and that significant repercussions of this experience are later to be heard in the Church Parables and in *Death in Venice*. What nobody realised, until Dr Mitchell made us aware of the fact, was that the history of Britten's creative encounter with the Orient – which began effectively *after The Turn of the Screw* – has itself a fascinating prehistory dating back to 1939 and Britten's friendship in New York with Colin McPhee, composer and authority on Balinese music.[28] Among McPhee's many published studies of Balinese music was a set of transcriptions for two pianos, four hands, entitled *Balinese Ceremonial Music*, which McPhee and Britten recorded for Schirmer's Library of Recorded Music. Apparently at that early stage Britten remained to be convinced that this music had anything to offer him from a compositional point of view;[29] yet the seeds were sown and, miraculously and no doubt unbeknown even to Britten himself, began to bear fruit almost immediately – in the harp textures of *A Ceremony of Carols* (particularly in the 'Interlude' for harp solo with its bell-like ostinato in harmonics and repeated use of the pentatonic scale), in the Sunday morning music in Act III of *Peter Grimes*,[30] in the harp's variation in the *Variations and Fugue on a Theme of Purcell* – and now, still in the pre-*Pagodas* era, in Quint's music in *The Turn of the Screw*. Why? Because Quint represents for Miles the opening of magic casements, a world of enchantment and glamour, of preternatural, supernatural, unattainable beauty. Tadzio represents the same world for Aschenbach in *Death in Venice*, and it is fascinating to watch a composer repeating himself under stress of similar emotions: particularly inasmuch as, whereas the gamelan stylisation in *Death in Venice* and in *Pagodas* are consciously done, this conjuring up of a similar sound world in *The Turn of the Screw* is just as surely unconscious, more subtle, and for this reason its genealogy has escaped detection these many years. But merely look at, listen to, the music in the night scene of Quint's first seduction of Miles and Variation VII which precedes it: the featured celesta flourishes (of which instrument much more anon), the harp tremolandos, the gong-strokes – all presage the Journey to Pagoda-land (Ex. 33). Also to the point is Wilfrid Mellers's observation that Quint's melismatic siren-calls to Miles recall flamenco music and Moorish cantillation – are, in a word, eminently unWestern.[31] The climax of Act I – the children lost in the night, held in thrall by the ghosts, deaf to the entreaties of the governess and Mrs Grose – grows a vocal/instrumental tissue of considerable complexity which is basically, however, an intensification to the nth power of the gamelan-like elements outlined in Ex. 33. The celesta figuration is now continuous and sensuously enmeshed in harp glissandos played to the same pentatonic tuning, the strings dissolve in a counterpoint of arpeggios, and Miss Jessel's gong-strokes set the entire texture awash in an unearthly glow and shimmer of sound –

Ex. 33

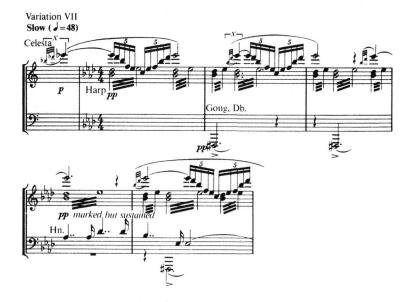

insidious and evil but also irresistibly beautiful. I use the water-metaphor advisedly, for the unmistakably watery quality of this ensemble – and what a fabulous fountain of sound it is – relates to the fact that this end-of-act finale is as much a sexual as a dramatic climax. Mellers (in *The Britten Companion*) calls it an 'orgiastic *ecstasis*', in more than one sense the high point of the opera; and of course the sound has to be other-worldly, unreal, exotic, since the scene can be interpreted as the product of the Governess's hallucinatory fantasy – and the character of the music surely hints at a similar fantasy-involvement with the children on the part of the composer himself. In my chapter 'Chaos and Cosmos in *Peter Grimes*' (*The Britten Companion*, pp. 108–19) I have discussed something of the significance in Britten of the water-music in such works as *Grimes*, *Billy Budd*, *Noye's Fludde* and *Death in Venice*; and it is presumably more than coincidence that Miss Jessel is always announced by the oozy, watery, oriental, black-sounding gong (with its overtones of death – and death in Britten is so often equated with sex, the sexual act being a plunge into the transcendence of Nirvana) and always appears to have risen from the depths of the lake – a creation of primordial slime, of the black womb and chaos of things. And when in their colloquy/soliloquy at the beginning of the next act the ghosts take as their motto Yeats's 'the ceremony of innocence is drowned', the reiteration of this line is accompanied by spurts and splashes of sound (upward-shooting harp glissandos and celesta arpeggios) and gong and cymbal strokes: all supported on an airy, undulating bed of woodwind tremolos. Again, pure gamelan; or rather pure gamelan-stylisation, the most important contribution to which is the celesta, a kind of substitute metallophone (Ex. 34).

Ex. 34

Ex. 34 (cont.)

This instrument takes us to the very heart of the opera by virtue
not only of the instrument it is and the sound it makes but also of the
actual notes it plays. That first 'tiny flourish' already referred to –
Miles dismissed his school – is in many ways a microcosm of the
whole work. Look for a moment at its immediate context. The key of
Mrs Grose's preceding aria – in which she muses contentedly on the
state of things at Bly – is a calm cloudless C major. Then comes
the celesta interjection, an intrusive Eb, as if in ironic response to
Mrs Grose's 'We were far too long alone' – well, they are to be alone
no longer. Mrs Grose's last note is an E, the celesta and the governess
both come in on an Eb – the third of the triad is lowered semitonally,
C major becomes C minor, light turns to night in an archetypal

Britten symbol (probably Mahler-derived) for the antithesis of good and evil; there is scarcely a work in which it does not appear in one form or another. It helps shape the profile of the all-important theme which Patricia Howard labels the 'catalyst' (see Ex. 16) a theme which, moreover, is of a melismatic, quasi-oriental caste; notice how the F♯ falls to an F♮, the E to an E♭. Nor is this all – far from it. Consider Ex. 34 itself again. The celesta, now: its sound is conventionally 'celestial', 'heavenly', 'other-worldly'.[32] But the ambiguity of the latter term is much to the point, for there are two other worlds, heaven and hell. Traditionally the celesta is associated with heaven; here it is the sound-symbol of its antithesis, hell, its tiny flourish the signature-tune of the Devil. A magic sound it certainly is; but the magic is black for all its ironic assumption of whiteness (the celesta's sound commonly described as 'silvery'). This ambiguity is central to the basic musical premises on which the opera is constructed. For if we examine closely not only the constituent notes played by the celesta in Exx. 33 and 34 but *all* its music, we shall find it unfailingly based on that archetypal musical symbol of innocence and goodness, of primordial nescience, the pentatonic scale; but here it is symbol of the *corruption* of innocence, of depravity and evil, of transcendent curse-of-consciousness. Further: everybody has commented on the fact that the 'Screw' theme embraces all twelve notes of the chromatic scale; but no one seems to have noticed the (to my mind) far more significant fact that those piled-up perfect fourths carry the strongest possible pentatonic implications and that, as a result, the entire opera is riddled with pentatonics – but pentatonics-gone-wrong, the so-called perfect fourths a musical incarnation of *im*perfection.

The pentatonic scale anyway has a built-in immutable euphony which has always rendered the chords derived from it – primarily the added sixth and ninth and minor seventh – very attractive to commercial musicians. These chords and the scale from which they are derived are particularly grateful to the ear, precisely because of the 'perfect' intervals which are pre-eminent in their make-up. Britten's harmonic fondness for the major second[33] is entirely due to the latter's pentatonic implications (so too is Debussy's, a composer who like Britten was greatly influenced by gamelan music and the oriental pentatonic scale). So Britten's use of this scale, with its 'great glow of freshness and purity' (to quote James's description of the children) in this 'wrong' context, with this positively negative aspect, can be interpreted not merely as a supreme irony but also as an elaborate blasphemy. It is perhaps scarcely an exaggeration to claim that, in Britten's *Turn of the Screw*, the entire *'natural' musical order of things is inverted*; 'inverted' being the operative (and in this case appositely loaded) word, since the result of inverting a perfect fourth is a perfect fifth, and what is the musical meaning of 'Quint' but a fifth? I am aware that this is in effect asking the reader to accept that the entire musical structure of *The Turn of the Screw* was motivated by a pun; and while I feel that Britten *must* have been aware of the musical implications of Quint's name,[34] I think it likely that they unconsciously, rather than consciously, influenced his choice of vocabulary. Whatever the facts of this matter, we should not be chary of recognising Britten's achievement (a) in creating a sense of all-pervasive evil through the very musical formulas normally and naturally (but there is nothing 'normal' or 'natural' about *The Turn of the Screw*) associated with all-pervasive good, and (b) in avoiding *totally* the cliché of the augmented fourth/diminished fifth, the conventional, traditional *diabolus in musica*. James's and Britten's devils are, however, neither traditional nor conventional. They are 'pets' and 'innocent babes', and their music has, necessarily, nothing to do with routine devilry and darkness either in terms of musical language or sonority, but everything to do with angels and light.[35] The music is thus in the profoundest possible way a positive complement to James's story. We are to meet this inverted symbolism again in Britten – in the Tempter's music in *The Prodigal Son* which incorporates Quint's celesta motif note for note (see Ex. 35) and in the explicitly oriental pentatonics of Tadzio's music in *Death in Venice* (Tadzio, another Angel from Heaven who is at the same time an unwitting Bringer of Death).

Ex. 35

The Prodigal Son

This inverting, or perverting, of the natural order is not confined to basic details of musical syntax and instrumentation, profitable though it will be to return to the latter in due course. It critically affects also, for instance, the Quint–Miss Jessel antithesis. In the

'normal' world we immediately associate a man with a low or bass
voice, the woman with a high or treble voice; the man with masculin-
ity, the woman with femininity, and any number of related sexual
stereotypes, most of them fairly meaningless anyway. Here, because
we are in an abnormal world in many senses (and homosexuality is,
by conventional standards, 'abnormal'), none of this applies. Miss
Jessel has the low voice and the low sonorities of the gong and
double-bass; Quint the high voice and high sonorities of celesta,
harp and (at one point) glockenspiel. There is nothing in the least
feminine or alluring about Miss Jessel: listen to her siren-call to
Flora with its atonal melodic profile (how ugly are those twisted
minor sevenths!) and ungainly rhythms which have the effect of
torturing and dislocating the child's name; how much more likely are
we to be wooed by Quint's sinuous, seductive arabesques with their
sybaritic oriental overtones, all concord and fluency (Ex. 36). Of this
Curst Pair of Sirens there is no doubt as to which one Britten (following James) intends us, no less than the children, to find the more
attractive.

Ex. 36

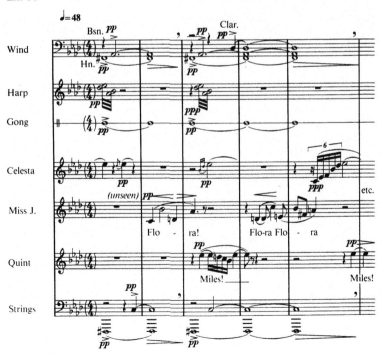

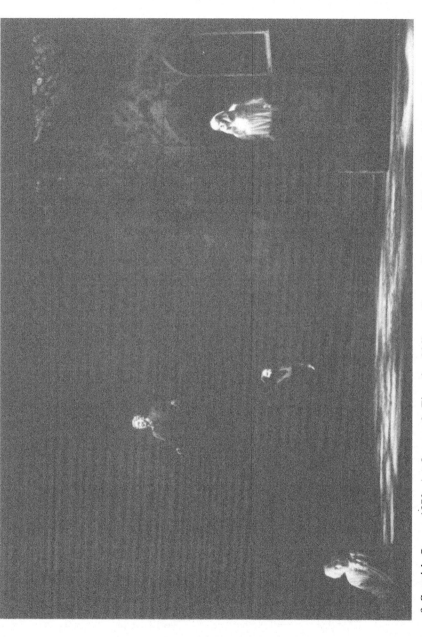

9 Scottish Opera, 1970, Act I scene 8. Timothy Oldham, Gregory Dempsey, Milla Andrew, Nan Christie. Producer, Anthony Besch; designer; John Stoddart.

It is symptomatic too of this reversed ordering of relations that Quint first appears on the height (on the tower), Miss Jessel from the depths (from the lake) and trails in insidiously closer and closer, one imagines leaving a slimy snail-like track behind her – a kind of variation on the hierarchical disposition of the characters in *Billy Budd*, the spiritual (as well as material) ordering of which places Billy at the top of the mast, Vere on deck below (both of them 'sympathetic' characters even though ironically each destroys each in his different way) and Claggart in the bowels of the deep, where monsters and the world's nightmares (Tennyson's kraken, for example, in the *Nocturne*) abide.[36] We almost feel a twinge of regret when Quint is defeated in the last scene, and wonder whether perhaps Miles would have done better to succumb to his blandishments rather than to the governess's neuroses.

The process of corruption of musical innocence begins almost from the start of the opera. There is immediately something sinister about the *Prologue*'s 'There had been a governess, but she had gone': the descending perfect fourth 'had gone' sounds less than perfect because of the unexpected intrusion of E♭ into C (cf. above, p. 108). Then the drum-ostinato of *The Journey* (pentatonic fourths again) has its worrying aspect (see Ex. 37). Ostensibly it represents the

Ex. 37

motion of the bumping, swinging coach bearing the governess to her destination (her Nemesis, as it turns out); but it also suggests a heartbeat (the familiar 'thumping heart' of anticipation) and, perhaps most important of all, carries primitive, barbaric overtones: even in the respectable respected seclusion of Bly, so far from the wide wicked world (it seems to say) things unheard of can be, the jungle is already thrusting upward, irrepressible instincts are lying in wait for man, ready to pounce on him and destroy him. (Are we not reminded of Aschenbach's vision of the jungle in *Death in Venice* with its attendant percussion ostinatos?) And Britten, ever a master of economy, sets all these reverberations in motion by dint of one percussion player with a handful of drums and pentatonic fourths at his disposal. We are inevitably (and I am sure intentionally) reminded of these jungle drums when the governess runs in on the scene of the children's night-*ecstasis* at the end of Act I to the sound of timpani beating out a derivative of 'Who is it, who?' and persisting in so doing until the end of the scene.

If we now turn from here to a later scene in which the fourths are featured in a transparently, at first sight conventionally, pentatonic manner – the sweet-summer music of Variation III, leading into *The Tower* – we will be startled to be put in mind yet again of *Death in Venice*, on two counts: (a) that in both cases the noxious potency of summer helps to precipitate a dire chain of events, and (b) that the figure on the tower who appears rudely to interrupt the governess's reverie is the exact counterpoint of the Traveller who disturbs (in more than one sense) Aschenbach in the cemetery: 'Who's that? A foreigner. . . how he stares. A rude, insolent fellow. I won't, don't want to notice him.' But for better or for worse Aschenbach *has* noticed him, and the marvels start to unfold, the 'wilderness swollen with fearful growths. . . strange hallucinations, inexplicable longings'. Is the latter not precisely the effect the apparition of Quint has on the governess? Immediately beforehand she has been deluding herself – or the pentatonic bird-calls over sustained chords have been deluding her – that the world is at peace. The summer evening scene is straight out of James – 'It was the first time, in a manner, that I had known space and air and freedom, all the music of summer and all the mystery of nature. . . the light faded, the last calls of the last birds sounded, in a flushed sky, from the old trees. . . I can hear, as I write, the intense hush in which the sounds of evening dropped.' The music transports us back to the Edenic stillness of the early-morning- and night-music in Act I of *Paul Bunyan* with its sustained pentatonic string chords and bird-song-like cadenzas for woodwind. Yet ironic undertones are everywhere to be heard: since Britten's bird-song, like Mahler's (and Messiaen's – and all three composers, in their different ways, found much to interest them in oriental music) is generally an emblem of Paradise Regained, or, rather, Paradise-Never-Lost.[37] Certainly the music convincingly registers Bunyan's 'sky that has never registered weeping or rebellion' (see Ex. 38). But, little by little, it is also quietly invaded by less comfortable nocturnal elements: fears flutter in the timpani (thrummed with fingers) and tremolo

Ex. 38

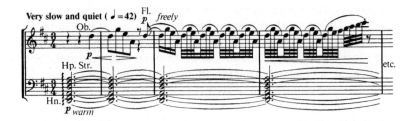

strings; the bird-calls become far-off cries in the night; and when the governess voices her wish that she could see *him* the cawing rooks (high bassoon over the cold and desolate sound of non-vibrato strings) assume a somewhat ominous aspect. Again, ambivalence is rife: for bird imagery occurs elsewhere in the score, and the birds in question are the reverse of *voces angelicae*. Quint tempts Miles with, among others things, the 'long sighing flight of the night-wing'd bird' (a marvellously set line, this, with its sighs and soft swoops in the vocal part – and later recalled no less marvellously as a quasi-heterophonic canon for the two violins in the cadenza sequence which opens Act II) and Miles and the celesta motif alike alight on Eb in echoing the key word 'bird'. Then, during Quint's altercation with Miss Jessel, he denies ever having called her from her school-room dreams: 'You heard the terrible sound of the wild swans' wings' – and, during the exchanges that follow, these wings continue to beat and flap in the orchestra in the form of one woodwind cadenza after another, each consisting of one melismatic phrase repeated freely and for as long as the singer needs to complete his line. (Britten's not-yet-invented 'curlew' sign, replacing the ⁀ , would have come in appropriately here, in every way!) The birds are no longer an emblem of innocence, un-knowingness, but of all-too-knowingness, corruption and terror.

The children's own music meets necessarily with a similar fate. After the governess has received the letter from Miles's school and she and Mrs Grose are wondering how he could possibly be accounted 'bad', the children are seen at the window quietly playing together and singing 'Lavender's blue'. The two voices remain in unison until the suggestive line 'While you and I diddle diddle. . . ' at which point they diverge in canon – and gradually die away, the phrase of the tune they have reached being picked up and completed by the 'white', 'pure' sonority of the harp but in glassy, spectral harmonics. It is, I think, a tiny masterstroke, that innocent, casual, slipping into counterpoint of the voices and their gradual fading out to the harp. *What* are they doing, *where* have they gone? It is all there, yet *not* there, in the music. The Hobby Horse scene, with 'Tom, Tom the Piper's son' is more unambiguously ambiguous, and capital has been made out of its sexual innuendoes in more than one production I have seen (see above, p. 37). Here the familiar nursery song is heard to go wrong in a more obvious way than 'Lavender's blue' - although the music has the heavy feel and pulse of a quick march the mandatorily regular bass accents are markedly irregular, the melody and accompaniment are perpetually at cross purposes key-wise, and the pig squeals and howls in the orchestra throughout.[38] The overall sound of the episode is not so much high-spirited as violent. Violence too is done to another archetypal symbol of childhood and innocence - church bells - in what we could call, after Mahler, the *Morgenglocken* scene in the churchyard (the combination of boys' voices and bells in the fifth movement of the Third Symphony is arguably the inspiration for this and many similar moments in Britten). The children's *Benedicite* in effect hymns (and invokes) not the bounties of the earth and the heavenly hosts but all the hierarchy of evil. Right from the start the chimes' F♯ major (the key, the 'sharpest' possible, was no doubt suggested by James's description of a 'crisp, clear day. . . the night had brought a touch of frost, and the autumn air, bright and sharp, made the church-bells almost gay') is undermined by the piano's intermittent semitonally trilling hum or drone (F♯ – G♮). The bell-pattern comes and goes at first, as distant chimes might on a veer of the wind; but when the governess tries to convince Mrs Grose of the children's 'otherness', their apartness from the 'natural' world, the bells begin to take an 'un-natural' interest in, begin to participate actively in, the scene; they set up a *pianissimo* but remorseless quaver ostinato on an A♯ with an acciaccatura G♯ before each note, i.e. a pentatonic major second. The governess foresees the children's destruction if preventive measures are not taken, and Mrs Grose urges her to write to the guardian. At this moment we are plunged, flash-forwarded as it were, into Pagodaland (see Ex. 39). Note the violin finger-tremolos, the quasi-gongstroke (piano and low strings) and, above all, Quint's pentatonic cluster in the chimes. Only now do we realise the direction in which that immediately preceding major-second ostinato has been pointing us: to Quint. Then Miles discovers how to divert the bells' motif

Ex. 39

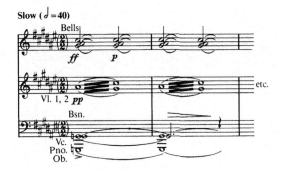

to his own purposes (see Ex. 40). Note the extraordinarily gamelan-
ish sound of the cluster-chord for chimes reinforced by piano (glissando across the tubes with the handle of the mallet).

Ex. 40

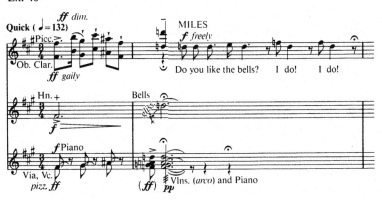

But the most chilling sound of all is reserved for the end of the
scene, after Miles has devastated the governess by challenging her to
take action. As he walks off into the church leaving the governess in
a state of total con-floption (to use an admirable East Anglian dialect
word which Britten would undoubtedly have appreciated), the violins, viola and high woodwinds (flute on piccolo) strike up a version
of the *Benedicite* tune which the children had first appeared chanting
(like choirboys) that is 'wrong' – masterfully – in every essential
respect (Ex. 41). The sharp key is un-natural for the strings anyway
(i.e. as uncomfortable as it could be, because it contains no open

Ex. 41

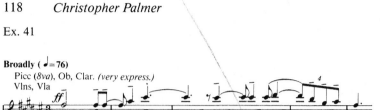

strings), the viola, clarinet and oboe are all taken up to heights unfit
for habitation (no composer in his 'right' mind writes a top F♯ for
oboe, so high a tessitura for clarinet can only sound unforced –
'natural' – if played on an E♭ instrument, and Britten specifies the
B♭); the unison itself is perverse – 'normal' practice would have been
to score such a line in two or even three octaves; and none of the
chords 'properly' fits the melody. The subtlety here is, as in 'Tom, Tom
the Piper's Son', that the alignment is always only slightly off target:
never crudely dissonant, but perverse enough to throw more than
one spanner in the heavenly works. Similarly in Miles's piano recital
scene the 'purity' of the Rococo pseudo-Mozart is quickly be-
smirched by polytonal clashes – even in the very first bars (from
fig. 84) the hands don't really fit together properly – and references in
the melodic line to 'Malo', Miles's own song, grow more persistent.
At fig. 95 the right hand brazenly asserts Quint's motif and his pentatonic (formerly celesta) roulades[39] – the pentatonic clusters of
F♯–G♯–A♯ have been leading us towards it for some bars – and at one
bar before fig. 96 a glissando down the black notes – how much more
pentatonic can you get than that? – effectively completes the casting
of the children's spell; with Mrs Grose asleep Flora can slip away to
join her companion. Miles seals his triumph (Variation XIV) by
emulating, on the piano, the fanfaring of ceremonial brass.

    The children's 'own' music – Miles's 'Malo' and Flora's lullaby –
calls for rather different comment since it is more directly expressive
of the children's being and is not a parodistic distortion of what is

familiarly associated with purity and innocence. Yet in other ways it is just as 'unnatural' – as indeed it must be, since the children themselves are, or are in process of being rendered, profoundly abnormal. The last instrument one would 'normally' connect with the clear daylight of childhood is the sombre, melancholic cor anglais; yet this is the colour central to the emotional resonance of 'Malo'. (Its impact is the greater for the instrument's not having hitherto been heard *at all* in the opera.) Flora's lakeside lullaby is no less oppressive, weighted down as it is with small cluster-chords in the harp which, towards the end of the lullaby, sink deeper and deeper by whole tones – as if not only pulling our eyelids down with leaden weights but also dragging us in to the depths of the lake, there to encounter a lurking Miss Jessel who materialises the moment the song is ended. (Her gong at fig. 65 seems to grow naturally out of the bass frequencies of the harp in the preceding bar.) It is in ways like this, and few yield all their secrets on a first hearing, that Britten drowns the ceremony of innocence.

As Eric Walter White has pointed out,[40] natural predilection as well as economic necessity influenced Britten in his choice of a chamber-music orchestration for *The Rape of Lucretia* in 1946. The ensemble consisted of string quintet, woodwind quartet (with various doublings), horn, harp and percussion – a dozen players in all – and went on after *Lucretia* to service both *Albert Herring* and *The Turn of the Screw*. This 'natural predilection' apart, there are two logical (and fascinating) reasons for the small-orchestra sound of *The Turn of the Screw*. The first is that the feeling of claustrophobia endemic to so many of Britten's operas, and particularly marked in *The Turn of the Screw* – indeed a protagonist, a key factor in the potency of the dramatic situation – is reflected not only in the all-conditioning, ubiquitous presence of the 'Screw theme', but also in the constitution and character of the orchestra. Twelve players working intimately together in the confined space of a theatre pit, each constantly aware of what his neighbours are doing, no big-symphony texture to mask or depersonalise – is this not in itself as it were one of those autonomous, enclosed communities which pervade Britten's life and work, his attitude to which was constantly ambivalent, and whose origins are to be found in his public-schooldays – a time of his life which in many ways he never outgrew? The chamber orchestra seen, in other words, as a musical microcosm of precisely that context which Britten found congenial, indeed indispensable to his sense of personal and professional well being, yet which posed problems to the attempted solution of which he devoted many of the best hours of his creative life (in *Grimes, Herring, Budd* and *Wingrave* as well as in *Screw* itself). Britten could well have equated the symphony orchestra with the big city, the chamber ensemble with the small town or large village which was his clear preference. Then secondly – and relatedly – a chamber-music texture has an openness, a candour, a sharpness and an essential *vulnerability* which again is a mirror image of what the opera is 'about'. Just as the child's mind perceives things in preternaturally bright colours and well-defined outlines, so the chamber ensemble has none of the symphony orchestra's tendency to blur and dim; it is an innocent as opposed to a sophisticate. Peter Evans has identified Mahler as the principal model for Britten's chamber-music orchestration;[41] and it is surely more than coincidental that the first work in which Mahler evolved his unique concept of chamber-orchestral scoring – the *Kindertotenlieder* – set a cycle of poems by Rückert, the burden of which is *the death of children and the loss of innocence*. These songs, composed in 1901–4, almost certainly show Mahler the *man* recollecting the feelings of Mahler the *boy* at the death of his much loved brother, Ernst, in early adolescence. 'It may well have been the case', claims Dr Mitchell in the most recent volume in his Mahler series, 'that it was with the *Kindertotenlieder* that the concept of the chamber orchestra was born in the twentieth century. . . one cannot really think of any work for small orchestra in the immediately preceding decades that is in any way comparable. . . what made history was the sheer refinement and elaboration of Mahler's orchestral writing. . . the degree of intensity of attention exacted from the listener'. Erwin Stein, who heard Mahler conduct the *Kindertotenlieder* in Vienna, recalled that the composer reduced the complement of strings to the absolute minimum, thereby no doubt achieving a sonority even closer in character to that of Britten's chamber operas. That this work was a powerfully determining influence on the lifelong character of Britten's instrumental thinking – and no one, I imagine, will want to dispute that it was – surely suggests that he was instinctively aware of the connexion between literary *matter* and musical *manner*, and adopted the principle himself. It is also worth noting that in other Rückert songs composed around the same time, Mahler begins to incline towards the pentatonic scale that was later to assume paramount importance in *Das Lied von der Erde* – its flavour is unmis-

takable in 'Ich atmet' einen linden Duft' (here too is 'Quint's' celesta –
but employed 'normally' to portray the 'heavenly' scent of linden
blossom) and in 'Ich bin der Welt abhanden gekommen'. Yet another
powerful link with Mahler in *The Turn of the Screw* is the prevalence
of night-music, for the origins of which we need look no further than
'O Mensch, gib' Acht' in the Third Symphony, the Rückert setting
'Um Mitternacht' (with its extraordinarily proto-Brittenian harp
cum piano – a novel sound in a symphony orchestra context); and,
above all, the final 'Abschied' movement of *Das Lied von der Erde*.
In all cases the orchestration has that always exposed, sometimes
reticently virtuosic, quality that Britten admired and emulated.

Mahler, then, must be taken due account of; but another conceivable model, much nearer home, has attracted less interest, namely
Holst. Britten's close personal and professional relationship with
Holst's daughter Imogen doubtless led to much familiarity on Britten's part with Holst's music, and Britten can hardly have failed to be
aware that Holst was one of the pioneers of chamber opera. In 1951
Britten made a version for the English Opera Group orchestra of *The
Wandering Scholar* (originally scored for a slightly smaller ensemble);
but the key work is *Sāvitri*, written, amazingly, as long ago as 1908.
It involves only three characters (plus a small off-stage chorus of
female voices); the orchestra consists of two string quartets, double-
bass, two flutes and cor anglais only (Holst, like Britten, was a
master of economic soloistic orchestration: the fewer instruments
playing and the more exposed their parts, the better); and Holst had
very definite ideas about the small-scale nature of the production.
The opera was to be given in the open air, or in a small building; no
curtain was necessary; no elaborate scenery was to be used, and the
'action' was to consist of no more than a few carefully controlled
gestures. Does this not read, in essential particulars, like an anticipation of Britten's Church Parables, the first of which was composed
some sixty years later? The common denominator is the Orient.
Holst, like Britten, was much interested in oriental thought, both
philosophical and musical; the fruits of the latter, thoroughly as-
similated, may be seen in such features as, in *The Hymn of Jesus*, the
free chanting of the 'Vexilla Regis' over an accompanimental figure in
strings and keyboards (celesta and piano together in a kind of proto-
gamelan sonority also employed by Mahler in the orchestral transition which leads into the *Chorus Mysticus* in the finale of the Eighth
Symphony) directed to be repeated ad lib until the chant is finished.

This passage clearly made a profound impression on Britten. I have already related the chromatic contours of Ex. 16, with its variable third, to oriental prototypes; and a recurrent motif in *Sāvitri* (see Ex. 42) employs this same significant interval with its ambiguous

Ex. 42

Sāvitri

Andante moderato
DEATH (*unseen*)

I draw nigh   to ful-fil my   work,

overtones. A paradoxical combination of austerity and sensuousness seems common to composers of this cast of temperament: we find it in Mahler and Messiaen as well as in Britten and Holst. What contrast between (say) the sweetly beautiful music for wordless female voices (a true 'heavenly chorus' since they are the concomitants of Death) and the dark severity of the chaconne-like passage which accompanies his slow advance and final retreat! And does the latter not also put us in mind of the *Turn of the Screw* denouement, cast in the form of a passacaglia? The link here is Purcell; the style of recitative Holst adopts in *Sāvitri* looks back to Purcell rather than to Wagner. Holst claimed that hearing the recitatives in *Dido* came as such a revelation to him that from then on one of his aims became to restore to the musical setting of English the kind of flexibility and freedom at which Purcell had been so expert.[42] Such was also, we need hardly remind ourselves, one of the chief aims of Britten. It is for these reasons that *Sāvitri* should not be overlooked as a precursor of *The Turn of the Screw*.

Most of us must be familiar with television series and plays in which the music – produced on a low budget – actually *sounds* low-budget; this at least has the negative virtue of making us appreciate all the more readily the consistently high order of expertise and imagination demonstrated in the scoring of *The Turn of the Screw*. Britten's string quartet never sounds like a quartet; in fact the overall sonority has that unity, that homogeneity, that sense of all-for-one-and-one-for-all, that is of the essence of great instrumentation. It seems almost as superfluous – even impertinent – to praise Britten for his orchestration as to praise Bach for his, so much a part is the colour of the total concept. It would also be superfluous (not to say laborious) to embark on a page-by-page description of the numerous ingenuities and felicities of instrumentation, since most of them are obvious enough to all who possess a pair of ears and/or a full score (preferably in that order of importance). I'd put, for instance, the children's music of bowing and curtseying in this category. It is also scarcely necessary to point out that each instrument is a soloist and must therefore be a performer of virtuoso calibre; for important solos abound from one page to the next, not merely in the cadenzas with which Act II opens. However a few subtleties are worth remarking. Certain string chords are unusually scored for special effect, for example at the governess's 'O why, why did I come', where the cello on the top note of the C♯ minor 𝄴 chord interjects a note of yearning and nostalgia. At Mrs Grose's 'You'll see soon enough' when the children are excitedly anticipating the governess's arrival, the top note of the chord (B♭ below middle C) is given to the double-bass and sounds downright sinister. One listens to the governess's 'Lost in my labyrinth' and receives the impression of hundreds of strings rushing, purposeless and panic-stricken, in all directions; one looks at the score to discover merely a few ordinary-looking chromatic scales, single instruments in unison or doubled at the octave, with here and there another instrument joining in for a couple of bars heterophonically to shadow the vocal line. No less remarkable is the fast *pizzicato* invention (mostly in three parts) based on 'Malo' in the scene in which Quint tempts Miles to steal the letter[43] the governess has written to the guardian. Britten reserves the *arco* for the climactic moment when the boy seizes the letter and carries it off to his bedroom. The score abounds in these simple but drastic – i.e., dramatic – changes of colour, one of the loveliest being the entry of the harp when the governess starts to read her letter aloud ('Sir – my dear Sir') in a G major with (pentatonic) added sixth. The warm, humanistic, *cantabile* quality of the strings in this much-admired passage is typical Britten; no less typical is his use of the woodwind to depict the non-human elements of pestilence and contagion – as they do, memorably, in *Our Hunting Fathers* and *Death in Venice*. Variation XI is a classic example, with the serpentine bass clarinet, alto flute alternately purring (deeply and hideously) and wooing and wheedling in bland and falsely lovely arabesque. A process of corruption is evidently under way in the bedroom scene which follows – but who is the corrupter and who the corrupted? For the glockenspiel (masquerading as the pentatonic celesta) indicates the presence of Quint. Somehow the clarinet – alto flute canon to which the governess plies her questions intensifies their prurience; here the very smoothness of *sound* is lubricious, although the actual sonority is that of the nocturne in Act II of *Albert Herring* and of 'Out on the lawn I lie in bed' in the *Spring Symphony*. In other words the 'sound' in itself must be neutral; what matters is the way we perceive it, and this is conditioned by the context *in* which we perceive it.

The famous and already cited line from Yeats – 'The ceremony of innocence is drowned' – seems to me to be the *fons et origo* of Britten's musical strategy throughout *The Turn of the Screw*: which is scarcely to be wondered at, since this is the theme, in the widest sense, of the opera itself. When we submerge an object in water its outlines and colours become nightmarishly distorted, and this is the process enacted in both drama and music in *The Turn of the Screw*. I have already commented on the subconscious sexual symbolism of this water imagery, and I feel that we miss a vital dimension of understanding if we fail to hear the opera in part as an expression of Britten's intellectual (i.e. his sublimated physical) paedophilia. The 'wetness' of that end-of-Act-I ensemble is that of infant, rather than adult, sensuality; and we cannot help wondering whether a 'normal' composer – Bliss, for example, whose knowledge and love of James must have been unparalleled among composers of his generation – could ever have rivalled Britten's delicate and tender way with his seriously disturbed characters, his peculiar insights into their behaviour and motivation. Few can have perceived the opera in this way when it first appeared some thirty years ago, and those who did had perforce to keep silent (a) because the composer was still alive and (b) because of the fact that homosexuality was still proscribed by law and any overt discussion of its artistic repercussions more or less proscribed along with it. Britten's generally somewhat bemused reactions to others' attempts to analyse or rationalise his work suggest that he himself was only partially conscious of the true nature of what he had created. Today we are in a much better position fully to comprehend the multi-layered complexities and ramifications of works like *Peter Grimes* and *The Turn of the Screw*. Philip Brett in his *Musical Times* article 'Britten and *Grimes*' (118 (1977) p. 955) was the first to bring Britten criticism out of the closet. In the postscript to his Cambridge Opera Handbook on *Peter Grimes*, he writes, 'the taboo on all mention of composers' sexuality was of course partly a manifestation of wider repressive forces from which all of us, straight or gay, need liberating. In the case of Britten it was also an affront to critical intelligence, for it tended to force those who write about Britten's music into evasive tactics verging on intellectual dishonesty or, even worse, into euphemisms . . . that were themselves oppressive and insulting' (p. 193). I have touched on these matters here, not, I hope, in any prurient spirit or from any urge to sensationalise, but simply because I believe, like Nietzsche, that 'the degree and kind of a man's sexuality pervades the loftiest reaches of his intellect' and that some knowledge of sexual make-up and motivation is an essential preliminary to understanding anyone – whether artist or no – on anything other than a superficial basis. But if one of the criteria of great art is its enduring quality (which consists in a work's ability to unfold new layers of meaning and relevance for succeeding generations), Britten did well to choose operatic subjects that were in themselves of great and urgent interest; or perhaps it would be truer to say that the subjects chose him. The operatic stage was Britten's medium for holding public discussion of certain basic human issues which touched him to the quick and his feelings about which he *had* to make known to the world. Music brings these matters into deeper and sharper focus (and, as an incidental but important advantage, how many of us owe our initial contact with such authors as Melville, James and Mann to Britten?), and one of the signal means by which it holds our attention is the sheer seductive quality of the sound, the magic of musical colour.

4 'The Turn of the Screw' in the theatre

PATRICIA HOWARD

1954. primer ✓

I Première

Many of the premières of Britten's operas are associated with festivals or notable events: *Peter Grimes* with the reopening of Sadler's Wells after the war, *The Rape of Lucretia* with the first post-war season at Glyndebourne, *Gloriana* with the Coronation and *A Midsummer Night's Dream* and the Church Parables making their first appearances at the Aldeburgh Festival. None, however, was launched on a more internationally prestigious occasion than the première of *The Turn of the Screw* on 14 September 1954 at the Fenice theatre in Venice during the biennial International Festival of Contemporary Music.

The occasion was not merely musically and socially significant. It was artistically congenial. Its well-funded luxury cushioned the frustrations of the normally inadequate preparation period which precedes most new productions. Basil Coleman, who produced the opera, relates that 'for once the fee for mounting this opera was adequate. It made possible a period of several weeks for the coaching, a month of rehearsals and for the singers to forgo all other engagements during the rehearsal time – a unique situation' (Coleman in Herbert (ed.), p. 41).

The cast for this production can be heard on the original recording of the opera:

✓Prologue	Peter Pears
The governess	Jennifer Vyvyan
Mrs Grose	Joan Cross
✓Quint	Peter Pears
Miss Jessel	Arda Mandikian
Flora	Olive Dyer
Miles	David Hemmings

126

Cross, Vyvyan and Pears were, of course, experienced interpreters of Britten's music. It was the casting of the children which raised problems. The auditions for the part of Miles were 'disappointing, leaving us with little choice. One of the boys brought back for a second hearing was a very shy but quite personable little twelve-year-old, with a true but very small treble voice. Despite this it was decided to risk casting him, in the hope that the voice would develop and grow during rehearsals' (Coleman in Herbert (ed.), p. 41). And in the event David Hemmings's Miles was widely applauded. Felix Aprahamian wrote of the boy's 'remarkable debut' (*Sunday Times*, 19 September 1954, p. 11), Reginald Smith Brindle was impressed by his 'fine musicianship and stage sense' (*Observer*, 19 September 1954, p. 15) and Virgil Thomson found him 'adorable all round' (*New York Herald Tribune*, 26 September 1954, section 4, p. 8). Most Mileses are. The part is so skilfully written that the most diffident acting and the smallest voice (provided that it is audible) are no handicaps to portraying this major character. Indeed, any such deficiencies can be turned into assets by a producer who channels them to enhance the aura of ambiguity and reticence which surrounds Miles.

The casting of Flora was and remains more hazardous. Basil Coleman recalls that having selected a Miles with a smaller voice than he had originally intended, 'Britten was more concerned than ever about the casting of Flora. . . it was finally agreed to cast an experienced adult singer who would be able to hold a sure vocal line, particularly in scenes which the child characters carry on their own' (Coleman in Herbert (ed.), p. 41). Critical reactions were mixed. In spite of Coleman's recollection that 'it is to the credit of Olive Dyer who played Flora, that some members of the audience asked to be taken backstage to meet the wonderful children' (p. 43), Virgil Thomson found Dyer 'neither convincing in movement nor vocally pleasing'.

Although the casting of Flora as an adult has remained the norm, it has continued to provoke unease. Anything which militates against the portrayal of the siblings as an *older* boy with a *younger* sister strikes at the heart of the work. It is important for James's story that Flora is a mere eight-year-old, both more vulnerable and more redeemable than Miles, and consequently with either a more certain prospect of a 'cure' or a more horrifyingly inescapable perdition. Louis Barcata thought that the fact that 'the work ends enigmatically with the girl Flora being taken away from the country house without

128

10 Kent Opera, 1979, Act I scene 7. Rebecca Platt, Meryl Drower. Producer, Nicholas Hytner; designer, Douglas Heap.

her giving up her obdurate connexion with Miss Jessel. . . is probably meant to indicate that woman, once tainted by evil, can never again be redeemed – an idea which fascinated Britten' (*Hamburger Fremdenblatt*, 18 September 1954, p. 6). But James is quite silent about Flora's fate, and it is as important not to know what becomes of her as it is to retain the more central conundrum of the governess's innocence. It seems that Britten never contemplated using a child singer for Flora[1] though the notable success of several girl Floras and especially the 1979 Kent Opera production, with twelve-year-old Rebecca Platt in the role, must lead to more girls being tried out in the part. The chief stumbling blocks for a child singer occur in Act I scene 7, where Flora's lullaby requires a flexibility of voice far more taxing than anything Miles has to sing, and the ensembles in Act I scene 8 and Act II scene 7, which need considerable power.[2]

The sets and costumes for the first production were designed by John Piper who had already worked with Britten on *The Rape of Lucretia*, *Albert Herring*, *Billy Budd* and *Gloriana*. The sets provide an ingenious solution to a multiplicity of problems. Basil Coleman outlines the requirements and describes the techniques:

The action takes place in no less than eleven different locales – mainly in Bly, a country house and its surrounding park, set in east England. The scenes are often very short, the orchestral variations in between even shorter, and this, together with the fact that the English Opera Group productions were conceived mainly for performance in medium-sized theatres and on tour, meant that large-scale or heavily-built scenery of any kind was not possible, even if desirable. How to melt in and out of each of the scenes effectively with the changes causing as little distraction as possible during the variations between? The difficulties were further increased by the virtual impossibility of achieving a good black-out on stage. In a chamber opera of this kind, and especially one which includes at least one child singer, the action must be brought downstage as much as possible, thus making it very difficult to make scene changes without them being visible in light reflected from the orchestra pit. In most theatres a gauze right across the proscenium opening throughout would have been a solution, but again the singers were anxious about not being heard or seeing their beat clearly enough. The idea had to be abandoned except on two occasions: for The Journey, the first scene of all, with the Governess travelling in a coach to Bly. As she got nearer her destination light faded up on the gauze in front of her, revealing the Gateway to the Park. A gauze was also used for the first scene of Act II with the ghosts of Jessel and Quint, where it helped considerably to create an illusion of 'nowhere' called for in the libretto.

John Piper and I decided to try to 'save up' units which together would suggest the facade of the house, only revealing them as the story unfolded and when they were needed for the action. For the first scene, entitled 'The Welcome', only the front door of the house was visible, placed downstage on one side, with a rather fully gathered gauze hanging across the stage beyond it, painted to indicate foliage and park. For the following scene, 'The Letter', the gauze was pulled off-stage to reveal a three-sided Victorian-Gothic bay window next to the front door. For the third scene another gauze pulled off-stage above the window unit revealed the tower on which the ghost of Quint would appear, thus completing the facade of the house on one side of the stage. Interior scenes were suggested by door and window units and pieces of furniture brought on from the opposite side of the stage and backed by further gauzes, one painted to suggest wall-paper for example. For the Churchyard Scene the church porch and tombstones were also brought on from this side. Throughout most later scenes we were aware of the Park and Jessel's lake painted on the backcloth with another painted gauze hung in front of it to give greater depth and mystery. . . Piper's response to Britten's operas is so sure that he has always found a way of realizing the essential texture and atmosphere of each of them in visual terms. *The Turn of the Screw* was no exception, and with the help of Michael Northern's clever lighting we got close to our original idea of making the scenes appear and disappear like a series of Victorian tinted vignettes, each lighting cue carefully timed with the music.   (Coleman in Herbert (ed.), pp. 41–2)

As producer, Basil Coleman's problems were mainly concerned with ensuring audibility (especially for Miles) and in making the ghosts ghostly enough.

When they were static, as on Quint's first appearance on the tower and Jessel's in the lake, the illusion was acceptable. It was much more difficult with a scene like the last of Act I where I felt it to be dramatically important that they should encroach nearer to the Governess and Mrs Grose in their desperate fight to keep a hold on the children. Even with different coloured lighting, the closer they came the more substantial they appeared. Yet, for musical reasons too, it was important that the singers should be near in order to help achieve the climax with which the act ends.

                                    (Coleman in Herbert (ed.), p. 42)

Several critics have identified the production technique as 'cinematic'.[3]

II Reception

Britten badly needed a warm and sympathetic response to his new opera. He wrote it while still distressed by the widespread critical rejection of *Gloriana*. Lord Harewood has suggested that *'Gloriana* together with its composer was under considerable attack at the time of its Coronation première, some critics, amateur rather than professional, deciding that it was an insult to the young Queen Elizabeth to show her ageing predecessor partly in a human rather than exclusively a regal light' (Harewood in Kobbé, p. 1487). But the rejection

11 Original production, 1954. Sketch for the final design by John Piper.

12 Original production, 1954. Set for Act I; designer, John Piper.

can be accounted for on a variety of fronts, and was not wholly rooted in the limitations of the first audiences. Professor Evans has given a scrupulously fair diagnosis of the comparative failure of the work: 'One suspects that the opera's first audiences felt cheated of another *Merrie England*, a sentimentalised picture of Elizabethan England adorned with vaguely archaic musical trimmings. But those who knew their Britten better may have been disappointed that he had relaxed so far the musical tensions that distinguished *Budd* as to devise a scheme in which set pieces are more patently isolated from their contexts than in any other of his operas, and in which the sonorous spectacle of tableaux is allowed to reduce the urgency of the action' (Evans, *The Music of Benjamin Britten*, p. 188).

These two views are written with hindsight. In 1953 Martin Cooper made an outspoken and perceptive analysis of Britten's relationship with his audience which recreates for us the critical climate of the mid-fifties and accounts for both the surprising venom of some of his detractors and the equally repellent over-protectiveness of some of his champions:

The reception accorded to *Gloriana* by the musical world in general – by which I do not mean composers or professional critics but the average intelligent music-lover and patron of Covent Garden as well as the gossips – marks a minor revolution in musical taste in this country. The work has been very generally over-blamed (as other of Britten's works have been over-praised) but with an almost sadistic relish or glee that has little to do with musical merit or demerit. The fact is that the fashion has changed and it is now smart to underrate Britten's music. This veering of public feeling was easily foreseeable. Whether he desired it or not, Britten and his music have been 'news' for something like ten years, a long run for any fashion; and nothing short of a spectacular success could prevent that fashion from changing. He has been ill-served, with the best of intentions, by a fanatical clique of admirers, whose exaggerated claims on his behalf have combined with an hysterical resentment of all critical comment to alienate large sections of the musical world. Finally, it has been felt that Britten has had the advantage of special patronage, special conditions of work and performance not accorded to other composers; and however much this may have been exaggerated, there has been much to give colour to the suspicion of a kind of 'most favoured composer' attitude in some influential quarters. This offends the sense of 'fair play' still very strong in the British public and has probably lent the note of bitterness to what might otherwise have been merely a change of musical fashion.   (Martin Cooper, *Spectator*, 19 June 1953, p. 783)

It was vital for Britten's self-confidence that *The Turn of the Screw* reversed the trend in popular fashion detected by Martin Cooper. And this it did with remarkable success. The international 'occasion' of the première exposed the opera to more disinterested criticism than any single work of Britten's had previously received. In a wealth of commentary from many nations, the doubts and reservations expressed by a handful of critics stand out as betraying isolated individual disagreements, reflecting the personalities of the writers more faithfully than the quality of the work under review. Britten, for his part, had returned to the stylistic tensions and masterly formal integration of *Billy Budd*. In devastating contrast to *Gloriana*, *The Turn of the Screw* is a work which exhausts by its concentration and economy — qualities which were perceived by the majority of the first-night critics. There were, for example, some outstandingly detailed analyses of the formal structure of the work, notably that by Colin Mason, who was the first writer to explicate both the structural techniques and their consequences for Britten's style:

With the possible exception of 'Billy Budd' it is in musical style the most difficult and tightly unified of Britten's operas. Technically, it carries this unification still further in the even more pronounced symmetry of structure and in that for the first time Britten consistently uses twelve-note technique. The opera is divided neatly into two continuous acts of eight scenes each, the scenes being all linked by orchestral variations on the twelve-note theme announced at the beginning of Act I. It would not be safe to assume from this that Britten had 'turned twelve notes', for the use of such a theme may, as has been suggested, have a special significance for this work – that it represents, by the revolution that (like all twelve-note rows) it undergoes before returning to the original note, the 'turn of the screw'.

Reduced to its most compact form of alternating rising fourths and falling minor thirds, it has in fact a screw-like movement, which might theoretically be continued indefinitely in the same direction as the alternation of two rising whole-tone scales a fourth apart. On the other hand, the actual title phrase never occurs in the opera, not even in the superfluous prologue (it would have been the one good reason for having it) and the theme may be interpreted as representing Quint, since in the last scene where the governess presses Miles to utter Quint's name, the theme appears in the bass in the orchestra, first eight notes, then ten, then eleven, and finally as he cries 'Peter Quint, you devil' the twelfth.

Britten no doubt meant this to be as ambiguous as James. What is perhaps more important about the twelve-note row is that its sequences of rising fourths allow Britten to establish and preserve classical tonality in the work, the more so by his layout of the theme, which, naturally, is not in its most compact form. His use of the note row is also very free, although it would not be an exaggeration to say that the entire opera is based on it. But what distinguishes the music above all is the variety of texture and invention and the unmistakable personality of Britten throughout it all.

The variations are not so-called for nothing, and it is often they that set the character of the scenes that follow. These, while even more closely integrated in style than in 'Billy Budd', are at the same time more varied and show, as in Britten's earlier operas and as again in 'Gloriana', his Verdian gift for devising vivid, memorable, and inexhaustibly varied accompaniments and figurations to adorn his simple melodic lines. There are a few pages in the work that have the kind of sound generally associated with twelve-note music, and many more that have not, but they are all alike in sounding like Britten. He has tackled yet another problem, brought off yet another tour de force, and, it seems likely, created yet another masterpiece.

(*Guardian*, 15 September 1954, p. 5)

I have quoted from this designedly ephemeral article at length because it seems to me to be an outstanding passage of 'morning after' writing – of analytical listening and immediate perception. Few other critics attempted such close scrutiny of Britten's structures, though many intuited that they were in the presence of 'not only Britten's most gripping score. . . [but] his finest' (Felix Aprahamian, *Sunday Times*, 19 September 1954, p. 11)

Some critics (for example Virgil Thomson) looked for and found the same lack of stylistic tension which had disappointed many of Britten's admirers in *Gloriana*. His lyrical approach, however, was widely commended, and brought him comparisons with Verdi (Colin Mason, Franco Abbiati) and Menotti (Virgil Thomson, and Luigi Pestalozza in *Avanti* (Milan), 15 September 1954) and the ambivalent adjective 'eclectic' was frequently applied to the style which both was and was not 'twelve note'.

The aspect of the work which came under greatest attack was Britten's deliberate choice of chamber forces for his orchestral support. Reginald Smith Brindle wrote that the 'wilfully sketchy orchestral score, eliminating the unessential to the nth degree, though dramatically adequate, is too bare and loose to satisfy'. Riccardo Malipiero was harsher, finding not only the 'customary poverty of chamber orchestras' inadequate to support the drama, but the whole role of the orchestral score too subservient, the music decorative and accompanimental rather than adding a layer of interpretation or commentary to the drama:

The subject, as we have said, is a morbid and yet a fascinating one which conjures up vast frescoes of sound, dramatic and dazzling structures full of zest and colour, and sound-images rich in meaning.
We had imagined a use of colour as an expressive force similar to certain effects which were successfully created in *Peter Grimes*. . . we hoped that Britten would have been equipped to contrast the overwhelming feelings of the protagonists with their child-like natures, and that he could have cast light on the tragedy which develops in these innocent souls, involuntarily corrupted. [Malipiero seems to cling exclusively to the 'first story' interpretation, a fact which might have rendered him less sensitive to the subtleties at the heart of Britten's score.]

There is, indeed, an expressive crescendo in this opera of only two acts for the second part is more intense than the first. Nevertheless, this crescendo, instead of rising to the peak of the harsh mountain of psychopathic revelation, stops short half-way and remains literal and narrative rather than musical and poetic. Admittedly many things are said on the stage and there is a denouement followed by the flight of the girl, and there is the death of the boy and the torment of the governess who wants to arrive at an explanation but who only succeeds in precipitating the tragedy; but all this has no musical equivalent except in a well-moulded vocal line. But can human speech, set to music, expound and illuminate the abysses of a soul which does not know delight or love but only fear and depravity? This must be the role of music, music designed as a connecting fabric, as illumination, as leaven to the drama. This, however, can only partly be observed in the second act, or rather in the first half of the second act. The whole of the first act, although its function is preparatory and therefore only potentially figurative, is nothing; the drama is lost in a notable vacuity of expression, in fluent but undistinguished invention, as is also the end of the opera which reverts to these mistakes after having touched some sensitive chords in the first scenes.

The conflict between infancy and degeneration could have been brought out better, taking advantage of the dramatic structure of brief, episodic scenes. There are indeed contrasts here and there but they are not related to the drama: they do not strengthen it – they only decorate it. The music is made a humble serving maid.

This is a mistake: Benjamin Britten has wasted a good opportunity and has wasted it perhaps partly through presumption. Is it not perhaps presumptuous to entrust the musical texture to an instrumental group of a dozen or so performers? Such things can only be done when each of the instruments achieves an expressive power such as few, very few musicians have attained up to the present day! Otherwise one risks the customary poverty of chamber orchestras!

While listening to this opera we were reminded of neglected examples of musical illusion – Bartók, Ravel in *L'Enfant et les sortilèges*, Berg in the lake scene in *Wozzeck* – examples, alas, which have evidently not served as models to be copied.   (Riccardo Malipiero, *Il popolo*, 15 September 1954)

This is an important criticism which I have attempted to answer in Chapter 3. But it stands alone in its widespread dissatisfaction with Britten's achievement. Abbiati wrote of 'a score which is a masterpiece of sound-images, skilfully thinned down to leave the statements and secret intentions of the characters completely clear'. Antoine Golea judged that 'with minimal means, with an orchestra of thirteen musicians and a remarkable lightness of touch, Britten succeeded in translating all the richness of Piper's libretto' (*L'Express* (Paris), 25 September 1954, p. 13). Barcata describes the paradox of a score which is at the same time both 'icy, cerebral and artificial' and also 'directed at the senses. . . It tries to plumb no depths yet the effects are sure, although they hit the solar plexus more than the ear. It is a delicate score, simultaneously muffled and shrill in sound.'

Much space was given in both the British and Continental press to debate what the anonymous critic of *The Times* disarmingly confesses to be 'an improper question':

We all know by now that Mr Britten's sheer musical ability is equal to any demands made on it, that his invention flows most readily from the inspiration of words, and that as a result of the combination of the two factors he accepts in song and opera the challenge of the most recalcitrant material. His operas in fact have generally provoked criticism to ask not whether he has succeeded in his aim but why did he choose this subject, that story or a particular libretto. It is an improper question for criticism to ask, but it recurs so invariably that it must have some relevance to his art.

(*The Times*, 16 September 1954, p. 9)

The perplexity of the Italian members of the audience at the 'morbid' subject occurs in many accounts of the première:

What should an Italian audience make of a sung version in the original language of a story which English readers have been reading for years without ever really finding out what it means?. . . Clearly their practice in Pirandello stood them in good stead, and they fell outside into dozens of little groups gamely, ingeniously, or obscurely explaining and counter-explaining, and all ready to die rather than look blank.

(Colin Mason, *Guardian*, 15 September 1954, p. 5)

By contrast, the professional critics competed to demonstrate their superior understanding of James – though it is curious (and an immense tribute to the opera's fidelity to James) that a plethora of conflicting interpretations was deduced by different members of the first-night audience. Virgil Thomson, for example, was convinced that 'both the libretto by Myfanwy Piper and the composer's musical treatment seem to have opted for that theory of the tale in which the ghosts are an invention of the Governess'. Reginald Smith Brindle, however, found that 'the haunting possibility dominating the book, told as it is by a neurotic governess, that her charges Miles and Flora are not corrupted by the apparitions of Quint and Miss Jessel, but that these are only figments of her own rampant imagination – that she herself, hallucinated, is the corrupter – has been obscured so that the real generator of suspense is lacking.' Malipiero, who commended the choice of subject for being in tune with the *Zeitgeist* ('our century is . . . a century of psychopaths, reflecting the psychopathy of art'), seems only aware of the 'first story', declaring without qualification that 'the minds of the children. . . have been contami-

avil = anlanmun.

nated by an evil serving-man and by a former governess, who are now dead but who continue to disturb the life of the innocents; in vain [the governess] attempts to win these poor souls back to normality'. Antoine Golea expressed different certainties:

Whether in Britten's musical treatment of James's themes one finds a classic ghost story or an anticipation of Freudian theories about the nature of dreams, it is evident that the composer's customary intense preoccupations – with homosexual love and the futility of struggling against it – are equally manifest in this work.

It is significant that whereas the girl Flora is ultimately saved from being possessed by Miss Jessel's ghost, the boy Miles succumbs to the attraction of Quint's domination. He dies in his governess's arms – she who tried her utmost to save him while being herself enslaved by a dark, unspoken passion for the young boy.

Louis Barcata, on the other hand, held that the opera succeeded in retaining all the ambiguities he recognised in James:

Sigmund Freud would have found this opera of consciously and unconsciously chosen, revealing dream symbols and abstruse references an interesting study. . . the swamps of the spiritual landscape in Myfanwy Piper's dramatisation of this ghost/detective story with a sexual–pathological background do not allow of any simplistic interpretations. . . at the end the question remains open whether the whole business is not simply a hallucination of the neurotic governess. There are no answers to such questions.

Whether Piper and Britten had faithfully recreated James's tale in the theatre has continued to be debated.[4] And the suitability of the subject matter for opera lingered as a topic for discussion at least in the columns of *The Times*.[5] But the story was quickly received elsewhere as splendid material for the opera house, including in its emotions and mysteries all the ingredients traditional to opera, with an unusual bonus for the producer: the opportunity to slant the production to favour either of two equally valid interpretations while not altogether obscuring the other, their coexistence being essential to a faithful portrayal of the source material.

A more leisurely and considered response to the opera has judged it to be one of the finest works Britten wrote. Lennox Berkeley's assessment is typical of the status now accorded the work: 'Berkeley considers *The Turn of the Screw* Britten's masterpiece; he thinks it is an almost perfect composition, which indicates a full flowering of Britten's gifts, and that it was the apex of the whole central period, the richest in its rewards' (Blyth, p. 44). Lord Harewood, however, has suggested that the gratifying reception accorded to *The Turn of the Screw* was not enough to compensate Britten for what the composer regarded as critical ill-will in the past: 'Harewood is certain that it was *The Turn of the Screw*, everywhere acclaimed as a great opera, that established Britten's reputation beyond doubt, but Harewood feels that it was one opera too late for him, as it were, to respond to public and critical acclaim; he wanted to do that after *Gloriana* – and he was spurned' (Blyth, p. 82).

III Stage history: performances since 1954

In his entertaining and appreciative review of the première, Virgil Thomson wrote that '*The Turn of the Screw*, words and music, is an opera that seems to me to have beauty and power in it. I predict it will travel.' His prediction has been fulfilled. The opera was, of course, composed with portability in mind. The original premiss of the English Opera Group was the 'creation of new works. . . capable. . . of being toured all over the country' (Britten, quoted in Kennedy, p. 47), and the Venice production was brought to London (Sadler's Wells theatre) in October 1954 before touring the United Kingdom in 1955.[6] That year the opera was also performed in the Netherlands (at the Holland Festival) and in Italy (the Maggio Musicale Fiorentino). In 1956 it returned to London (the Scala theatre), and in 1957 it was given at the Royal Opera Stockholm and the *Landestheater* in Darmstadt. In 1958 it reached Tokyo in April and Montevideo in August. After two years in which new productions are absent, the work seems to have circulated with greater vitality than before. In 1961 performances included the Oxford University Opera Club, the Aldeburgh Festival, the Boston Arts Festival, the Rosehill theatre at Whitehaven, Cumberland, and the *Teatro de Opera de Cámara* in Buenos Aires. In 1962 it returned to Sadler's Wells and was also performed in New York, Edinburgh and Zurich. In 1963 it was given in Salzburg and in 1964 the English Opera Group took it on a European tour which reached Moscow in October – the first British opera company to perform there since the 1917 revolution. The work was also featured during the 1964–5 season at Marseilles. In 1966 numerous performances included notable new productions in February by the Morley College Opera Group and in October by the London Opera Group. In 1967 it was given at Gelsenkirchen (near Essen), in Copenhagen and in Stockholm. In 1968 it was performed in Milan, Helsinki, Tours and at the University of New South Wales. In 1969 it was given by the Opera Society of Washington. The year 1970 saw, in addition to a new production by Scottish Opera, two productions in

Rome. In 1971 the English Opera Group mounted a new production, which was given at the Maltings, Snape, during the 1972 Aldeburgh Festival. In January 1972 the opera had returned to the Fenice theatre in Venice for the first time since its première. In 1973 Scottish Opera took their production to Lisbon, and the opera was also performed in Sweden, Antwerp and Geneva. There were student productions at the University of Exeter in 1973, the South East Derbyshire College of Further Education in 1974 and the Juilliard School in 1975. Other performances in 1975 included productions in Chicago and Texas. In 1976 the English Opera Group, re-formed as the English Music Theatre Company, took the work to the Brighton Festival. A new production was also given at the Wexford Festival in the same year. The year 1977 saw performances in Łódź and Warsaw; 1978 was a particularly strong year for the opera, with a production in Vienna in March and performances by Scottish Opera in Zurich in May and Frankfurt in June; new productions in London include those by the Barbican Opera Group in June, a student performance at the Royal Academy of Music in July, and the Studio Opera Group in September. A new production was also featured in the 1978–9 season by the Welsh National Opera. The work was equally well served in 1979 with performances in Hanover in the summer, at the Edinburgh Festival (Scottish Opera) in September, and two new productions in the autumn by English National Opera and Kent Opera. In 1980–2 it reinforced its world-wide reputation with productions in Geneva (1980–1), St Louis (1980), Tokyo (1980), and Stichting (1981–2), while in the same years student productions were given by the University of Hull (1981) and the Royal College of Music (1982).

It is a remarkable record for any contemporary opera, offering abundant testimony to both the effective practicality of the work in the theatre and its widespread and enduring appeal. However although *The Turn of the Screw* has attracted some of the greatest conductors and producers of our time, subsequent productions have remained remarkably close to the experience of the first performance.

IV Production: some options

The reasons for this lie in the score itself. The stage directions, as we have noticed in Chapter 2, carefully define the areas of ambiguity in the relationship between the ghosts and the children. And revisions to the libretto (see Chapter 2 note 10) seem designed to tighten up the definitive staging of the opera. If these directions are followed to the letter, Flora, for example, does not see Miss Jessel in Act I scene 7, and is seen by the audience not to see her. And Quint remains off-stage in Act II scene 4, so that his voice can be interpreted as sounding either in Miles's head or in the governess's.

The most significant changes in staging are those which producers have introduced in order to remove impartial ambiguity, and to bias the interpretation towards either the first story or the second. As early as 1956 Basil Coleman's production was altered slightly to give the ghosts less objective reality: the critic of *The Times* recorded that 'in the first scene of the second act, where rather dubiously the ghosts become solid flesh, they no longer act so physically and their colloquy remains in the realms of shadow' (27 September 1956, p. 5).

A much bolder step along the same road was taken by Geoffrey Connor in his closely-interrelated productions for Morley College (1966), the Royal Theatre in Copenhagen (1967) and for Danish television (1968). Connor believes that the first performances of the opera had an inappropriate simplicity about them, amounting to an innocence of approach which belied the intrinsic intensity and subtlety of the score. He found Coleman's production too straightforwardly committed to the 'first story', and has suggested that Britten's response to the ambiguities and ambivalences in James's tale may have been at an unconscious level, so that the composer himself was not fully aware of the richness of his own work when he collaborated on the first production.

Geoffrey Connor believes that this is also true of *The Rape of Lucretia* and *Billy Budd* – operas which the original productions presented in terms of black and white: the absolute innocence of the victims Lucretia and Budd and the total evil of their destroyers, Tarquinius and Claggart. As these works have become more familiar, greater depths have been discovered in them, so that it is possible to present a Lucretia who yields to a deeply suppressed desire for the charismatic villain, and a Claggart who is as much a victim as Budd – both of them suffering under the social and hierarchical tyrannies under which they lived. The bases for these later insights are in the scores themselves and were surely present at some level of Britten's consciousness. Clearly the producer has a crucial role to play in teasing out the full values of these works:

My work on *The Turn of the Screw* stemmed from an earlier production of *The Rape of Lucretia*. I was present at the early rehearsals and performances at Aldeburgh of *Lucretia* and was moved by the beauty of the music and the poetic imagery of the text. I also shared the widespread disappointment at the unconvincing dramatic ambience of the work and its moral conclusions, weaknesses that were always laid at the door of the libretto of Ronald Duncan. For me, Duncan had created a poetic text suggesting an appropriate timelessness (rather like Maeterlinck's *Pelléas et Mélisande*) and deserved greater recognition than he seemed ever to have publicly received. The main problem lay rather in the nature of the dramatic conflict as envisaged by Britten.

Here was the first example of what was to prove to be his instinct to reduce all human passions to abstract duels between Forces of Evil, often left undefined but hinting at the sexually repressed, and Forces of Good, often of the implausibly good. *Lucretia* was only the first example of this Brittenesque tendency to dramatic abstraction which we would see run through all the succeeding operas up to the final desolation on the Lido at Venice, and it is this abstraction rather than the small-scale nature of the works which in my view was to prove the main hindrance to their complete acceptance in the main repertory. Presenting the operas in the theatre, one has to find ways of imbuing them with dramatic vitality so that the situations match the fine, nerve-exposed music. Goodness cannot engage our sympathy unless it comes off its pedestal and Evil will not command our interest – not to mention the best tunes – unless it acquires a D and becomes identifiable.

I had the opportunity of developing these ideas at Morley College with a production of *The Rape of Lucretia*, the first by a company other than the English Opera Group. Lucretia had to be lovingly brought down to earth and the two Chorus figures had to be recognisable people instead of pious oracles from Golgotha. The generalised moralising that had so strongly dominated the work was thus much reduced. The rape and its associated violence could be related to characters of flesh and blood; the commentaries and final benediction of the Choruses accepted as balm to their bruised lives and, as in all good theatre, the audience could be trusted to related what it had seen to its own life.

The next Virtuous Heroine was the Governess of *The Turn of the Screw* and, as was evident from the stage directions in the vocal score and the first production, we were meant to accept the Ghosts as being real, the Governess as fighting a lone battle against Evil and the once innocent children now corrupted. Again, in spite of an imaginative libretto, the masterly, tortured music was tied to a Brittenesque conflict in which the Ghosts were not the only characters lacking red blood. However, by turning as sceptical an eye on the Governess of the opera as had already been turned on Henry James's original lady and her story, the blood quickened on both sides of the proscenium, the stage stirred to recognisable life and music and action became one. This shift of emphasis left intact the ambiguity of the original tale. James's story and Britten's music tell of the disturbing reality of human actions under stress. In such a context real ghosts appear to be merely frivolous, reducing something rare and penetratingly true into just another ghost story.[7]

'Where this production scored over that by the English Opera Group is in restoring the ambiguity of James's original story so that at the end we were rightly left wondering whether Quint and Miss Jessel are "real" ghosts or merely figments of the Governess's very vivid imagination.' (Alan Blyth, *Guardian*, 25 February 1966). Geoffrey Connor succeeded in restoring an awareness of the 'second story' by focusing the opera continuously on the governess. His most important innovation was to have the governess on stage during the Colloquy in Act I scene 1, permitting the interpretation that this scene takes place in her imagination only – and investing her admission in the Soliloquy which follows with a new and ominous significance:

I know nothing of evil yet I feel it, I fear it, worse – imagine it.   (II. 1)

In his production for television Connor was able to take this process further by using the variation interludes to probe and illustrate the governess's alternating moods of insecurity, over-confidence and frustration. In particular, he exploited Variation VIII, which opens Act II with a sequence of instrumental cadenzas recalling music from Act I scene 8, *At Night*. During this variation Connor showed the governess reliving in her own mind the events of the earlier scene. This interpretation removes the stumbling block we noted in Chapter 2 – the unease expressed by some critics that Act I scene 8 is too crude and definite a realisation of events which in James are presented as groundless suspicions. Connor's use of television techniques restored these events to their authentic theatre: the governess's mind.

Geoffrey Connor's ideas proved to be seminal, and a number of subsequent productions can be traced to their influence. Coincidentally, and without having seen Connor's production, Anthony Besch adopted a related approach in his production for Scottish Opera (1970), where again the governess was present throughout the Colloquy, 'her head wrapped in a halo of light' (John Higgins, *The Times*, 3 April 1970, p. 12) while Quint and Miss Jessel converse in her imagination. The starting point for Anthony Besch's approach to the opera was a conversation with Erwin Stein during the early stages of the opera's conception in which Stein revealed that Britten was convinced the ambiguous phrase, 'Peter Quint, you devil!' (Act II scene 8), was addressed to the governess – a sure indication of the 'second story' interpretation. However, when he saw the first production, Besch felt that many of the intrinsic ambiguities of the story had been rejected in favour of an almost exclusive 'first story' interpretation. His production set out to restore the balance, and to leave the audience with an unanswered question about the nature of the evil at Bly. It was important to Besch to establish exactly how limited was the evidence for the objective existence of the ghosts. His production made clear that the governess never hears the ghosts and that the children never see them. And he restored what, on Stein's evidence, was Britten's initial response to Miles's last words – the child's unambiguous indictment of the governess.

Besch's production also attempted to illuminate the governess's relationships with her employer and with Quint. As we have seen (Chapter 2, p. 36) he used the *Prologue* to show a mimed encounter between the governess and the guardian, while the 'Douglas' of James's story sang the narration. The guardian was acted by the singer who was later to play Quint, and he displayed similar physical characteristics in both roles. The intention of this bold innovation was to show how Quint and the guardian were to become confused and rival obsessions in the governess's mind. The connexion between the characters is memorably forged in Act I scene 4, *The Tower*, and by letting us see the guardian in the earlier episode, Besch allows the audience to experience some of the governess's sense of shock, disappointment and even disgust at seeing this distortion of the man with whom she was infatuated. Her concentration on Quint (and through him on Miles), the improbability of which we noticed in Chapter 2, p. 39, then becomes plausible, and the torment of the governess's unrequited passion becomes the mainspring of her tragic hallucinations. It is a telling corroboration of this insight that when the governess imagines Quint and Miss Jessel together (in Act II scene 1), she conjures up a scene in which Quint spurns Miss Jessel as heartlessly as she feels she has been spurned by the guardian.

Many producers have chosen to weight the opera in favour of the 'first story', however. Among these, Vic Dowdall's production for the London Opera Group (1966) focused on Quint's struggle to possess Miles, showing him dependent on the child to win some kind of release: throughout Act I and during the Colloquy Quint appeared in fetters, which fell off when Miles stole the letter in Act II scene 5. The whole of this production was slanted towards the objective reality of the ghosts. Flora clearly registered the presence of Miss Jessel in Act I scene 7, and Quint appeared physically to Miles (and to the audience) in Act II scene 4. As Joan Chissell pointed out, 'ghosts so prominent and active, leaving little to the imagination, paradoxically reduced the eeriness of the piece' (*The Times*, 13 August 1969, p. 12).

It is, though, important for the continued vitality of an opera that experiments should continue to be made, even if they sometimes misfire. An opera can become embalmed in its own stage traditions, and *The Turn of the Screw* offers fewer options to producers than many operas, not just because of those very specific stage directions but because of the extreme tightness of the intrinsic structure of the work: the content of each scene is exactly defined both by the highly organised music (the very moment of the appearances of the ghosts, for example, is literally orchestrated into the score) and the precision of the evidence which each stage in the story offers. An area, however, affording a wide field for reinterpretation is the degree of realism to be attempted in the scenery.

This turned up as a problem in the first production:

at the first arrival of the Governess at Bly, [Britten] had already sketched 'arrival' music, before points of production had been decided. He said: 'Look, when she arrives, obviously she didn't come by train, she came by coach or something, a wheeled vehicle you see, at any rate to the outer gate at Bly. We must have a coach.' In the end there was no coach: the coach music (or coach-horse music) is so vivid and telling that a coach is simply not necessary, and he was finally convinced of this.

(John Piper in Herbert (ed.), p. 6)

There have been coaches in many subsequent productions and this issue does not seem to be a crucial one, though it is symptomatic of conflicting attitudes towards the options of realism and suggestion in the scenery which do seem to impinge on the interpretation of the opera. Within an essentially realistic convention, John Piper's original conception, with fragmentary 'solid' areas (the door, the window, the tower) linked by areas of darkness accentuated the dream-like and the remote (see Plates 11 and 12). At the other extreme, Adrian Slack's production for Welsh National Opera (1978) was notably well furnished with substantial brick surfaces much to the fore (see Plate 4). Most realistic sets lie between these two extremes, though the producer's choices are often influenced as much by the peripatetic customs of the company as by his imaginative concept. For Nicholas Hytner's highly mobile Kent Opera production of 1979, for example, the set was even more minimal than Piper's:

the acting area is reduced to the front of the stage, the remainder being cut off by white sheeting, which draws upwards to permit basic props (a doorway and wall, for example, or a table and chairs) to revolve into place and through which Quint and Miss Jessel are mostly seen.

(Stanley Sadie, *The Times*, 18 April 1980, p. 11)

The effect of this sparse production was to maintain a more formidable barrier between the ghosts and the human characters than is cus-

13 Kent Opera, 1979, Act II scene 2. Sam Monck, Rebecca Platt, Margaret Cable, Meryl Drower. Producer, Nicholas Hytner; designer, Douglas Heap.

tomary; at the climax of Act II scene 8, a bigger-than-life-size silhouette of Quint surged up against the backcloth, now on one side, now on the other, so that the terror he evoked was intensified by a fear that he would actually break through the sheeting and invade the stage. A production, however, which aims to etherealise the ghosts by keeping them locked behind gauzes throughout has to compromise in Act II scene 3, where there is no option to having Miss Jessel in the schoolroom, at the desk, as large, as it were, as life. No production has managed to make the ghost a less than fully physical presence here.

A different approach to the supernatural is to make no difference between the human and the supernatural characters but to invest the set with such a degree of unreality that doubt is cast upon the truth of the entire sequence of events acted out on it. This was the premiss of Colin Graham's production (English Opera Group 1971, revised in 1976 for the English Music Theatre Company). Yolanda Sonnabend's set was stark and symbolic. As in Kent Opera's production, the acting area was limited, but this time to a circular area – any such deliberate demarcation of a part of the stage tends to exclude a wholly realistic interpretation and emphasises the theatrical frame. The structures were sparse but full of significance, notably the twin ash saplings which framed the acting area, standing for the two children and evoking a rich supernatural folklore tradition. The slab on which the governess slept in Act II scene 1 was revealed in Act II scene 2 to be a tombstone and became Miles's bed in Act II scene 4 – eminently practical transformations but full, too, of morbid significance. The ghosts were not distinguished from the human characters either by make-up or costume (William Mann commented, 'some might not appreciate that they are spectres at all' – *The Times*, 10 May 1976, p. 12), and the production fostered a nightmare atmosphere, with every gesture and inflexion used to emphasise the hysterical possessiveness of the governess, from which, we were invited to believe, the whole drama sprang (see Plate 14).

A still greater degree of abstraction and harsher images were evoked in Dacre Punt's designs for Geoffrey Connor's production for Morley College and Copenhagen (see above). In these, structures of steel rods and movable wire mesh panels 'could represent objects and surfaces or merely hint at the layers of complexity in the opera (or the human mind). And the semi-abstract backcloth could suggest anything from the green innocence of spring to the most horrific sexual symbolism' (*The Times*, 24 February 1966, p. 16) (see Plate 15).

14 English Music Theatre Company, Snape 1976; set design by Yolanda Sonnabend.

15 Royal Theatre Copenhagen, 1967; set design by Dacre Punt.

To date there has been a marked, though surely not inevitable, correlation between the degree of abstraction of the set and the psychological intensity of the performance. Certainly in comparison with Colin Graham's and Geoffrey Connor's productions, one which is played out before a wholly realistic set can seem inappropriately relaxed. Jonathan Miller's recent production for English National Opera (1979) featured a spacious realistic set (and coincidentally in Michael Ginn one of the most diminutive of Mileses). William Mann interpreted Miller's intentions as being 'to bring home the apparent physical vastness of a child's surroundings, and thus suggest how hardly children's curious behaviour will be comprehended by elders who have forgotten the relative dimensions of childhood' (*The Times*, 10 November 1979). The set, designed by Patrick Robertson, dominated this otherwise somewhat noncommittal production, both by its beauty and its fidelity to James's atmosphere – presenting the sunny along with the sinister, as more static settings are usually unable to do (see Plate 16). Patrick Robertson's work in the theatre has made a special feature of projections. His set for *The Turn of the Screw* employed 'three stepped panels on each side of the stage. . . of expanded aluminum grill, which could register both frontal and rear projections in a sharper, harsher manner than fabric or folio screen. Narrow semi-mirrored panels filled the gaps between the large panels. Consequently one could also see through the entire onstage walls and view a set of opaque panels behind them. . . Many combinations of projections were possible as a result, including startling and eerie transformations as one shifted from one surface to another, or from frontal to rear projection, all of which was quite appropriate to the ghost story libretto of the opera' (Jarka M. Burian, *Theatre Design and Technology*, Fall 1983, p. 4). The resulting kaleidoscope of exterior and interior scenes at Bly cleverly reduced the acting area to a space appropriate to the intimacy of the score, while retaining the full depth of the Coliseum stage for certain effects. It was not a set to question reality (as Yolanda Sonnabend's clearly intended) let alone to deny it (as in Dacre Punt's designs) but to show, perhaps, how the real world can play upon vulnerable imaginations: Miller's production implies that there is enough in the numinous beauty of the English countryside, in the secret life of a large, old house, and in the unbridgeable gulf between childhood and the adult world to raise a ghost or two. Patrick Robertson's set remains the one visual concept of the opera which an admirer of Henry James, knowing nothing about opera, would recognise as faithfully reproducing the strong visual suggestion of the story.

16 English National Opera, 1984, Act II scene 2. Nicholas Sillitoe, Rosanne Brackenridge, Margaret Kingsley, Jill Gomez. Producer, Jonathan Miller; designers, Patrick Robertson and Rosemary Vercoe.

Notes

1. Henry James's *The Turn of the Screw*

1 Edmund Gosse's anecdote quoted by Leon Edel (ed.), *Henry James: Stories of the Supernatural* (London, 1971), p. 426. Letters to H. G. Wells and F. W. H. Myers: *The Letters of Henry James*, ed. Percy Lubbock (London, 1920), 1, pp. 306, 308. 'Christmas-tide toy': Henry James, *The Art of the Novel: Critical Prefaces*, with an introduction by R. P. Blackmur (New York and London, 1962), p. 170

2 *The Notebooks of Henry James*, ed. F. O. Matthiessen and Kenneth B. Murdock (New York, 1947), pp. 178–9

3 James on Wilkie Collins: review of Miss Braddon's *Aurora Floyd* (1865), reprinted in *Notes and Reviews*, ed. Pierre de Chaignon la Rose (Cambridge, Mass., 1921), p. 110. Comment to Sir James Mackenzie quoted in Leon Edel, *The Life of Henry James* (Harmondsworth, 1977), 2, p. 256

4 On Peter Quint as George Bernard Shaw, see E. A. Sheppard, *Henry James and 'The Turn of the Screw'* (London, 1974). On James's association with the Psychical Research Society, see Francis X. Roellinger, 'Psychical Research and "The Turn of the Screw"', *American Literature*, 20 (1949), pp. 401–12.

5 On James's possible knowledge of contemporary psychological theory, see Oscar Cargill, '*The Turn of the Screw* and Alice James', *PMLA*, 528 (1963), 238–49.

6 *Ibid.*

7 Quoted in Simon Nowell-Smith, *The Legend of the Master* (London, 1947), p. 49

8 Myfanwy Piper, 'Writing for Britten' in David Herbert (ed.), *The Operas of Benjamin Britten* (London, 1979), p. 12

9 Henry James, *Partial Portraits* (London, 1888), p. 406

10 Henry James, *The Turn of the Screw and Other Stories* (Harmondsworth, 1969), p. 46. All the pages references relate, throughout the book, to this edition.

11 *The Independent* (5 January 1899), p. 73; *The Bookman* (November 1898), p. 54; *New York Times Saturday Review of Books and Art* (15 October 1898), pp. 681–2; *The Outlook* (29 October 1898), p. 537; *The Critic* (December 1898), pp. 523–4

12 *The Letters of Henry James*, 1, p. 306

13 See Robert Heilman, '"The Turn of the Screw" as Poem', *University of
Kansas City Review* 14 (Summer, 1948), pp. 277–89; Dorothea Krook,
The Ordeal of Consciousness in Henry James (Cambridge, 1963),
Chapter 4.

14 *The Letters of Henry James*, 1, p. 305

15 *Ibid.*, p. 308

16 Edmund Wilson, 'The Ambiguity of Henry James' (1934), reprinted in
The Triple Thinkers (London, 1952), pp. 89–128

17 *The Novels and Tales of Henry James*, New York Edition (London,
1909), 12, p. 308

2. Myfanwy Piper's *The Turn of the Screw*: libretto and synopsis

1 Letter from Mrs Piper to the author, 22 February 1982. See also Anthony
Besch's revelation, Chapter 4, p. 142.

2 Though this is not the only way of staging these scenes. Some alternatives are discussed in Chapter 4.

3 The chamber operas were written for the English Opera Group, formed
in 1946 with the aim of stimulating 'new works performed with the least
possible expense and capable of attracting new audiences by being
toured all over the country' (Britten, quoted in Michael Kennedy, *Britten*
(London, 1981), p. 47).

4 This suggestion was made after Basil Coleman's 'bombshell'; see p. 64.

5 Purcell's *Dido and Aeneas* and Gluck's 1762 version of *Orfeo* are among
a number of operas neglected chiefly because they do not fill an evening
at the opera. *The Turn of the Screw* remains a short opera, running at
well under two hours. (The original recording takes 1 hour 46 minutes.)

6 All references to the libretto are identified by act and scene, and are taken
from the definitive version of the libretto, published in *The Operas of
Benjamin Britten* by David Herbert (ed.), pp. 233–48. This libretto differs
slightly from an earlier version published in the booklet accompanying
the recording of the opera in 1955, and also from the version in the vocal
and orchestral scores. Where these variants are of interest the several versions are discussed, for example in note 10.

7 Act I scene 6 is based on hints in James's Chapter 9 but no such single
scene occurs in the story.

8 The libretto places the final scene in the grounds, with Quint's last
appearance initially on the tower. This allows for an extra thrill of terror
when Quint descends the tower to claim Miles, but the intimacy and
intensity of Miles's relationship with the governess is perhaps better communicated in an interior scene. In James it is the dining-room window,
not the window of the schoolroom, at which Quint appears.

9 J. Purdon Martin, 'A Neurologist's View', published in the programme
booklet for the English National Opera's production in November 1979
(no page numbers)

10 This quotation is taken from the stage directions in the vocal score on
pp. 76–7. In the definitive libretto (see note 6) the wording is a little
different:

When the song is over she goes on fussing over the doll as she murmurs the last two or three sentences, until Miss Jessel appears on the other side of the lake. Flora silently and deliberately turns round to face the audience away from Miss Jessel. (I. 7)

This wording does not, perhaps, *necessarily* preclude Flora's glimpsing Miss Jessel before she turns, though producers rarely allow her to do this. A similar point could be made about Act I scene 5 in which the earlier version of the libretto published in the record booklet provides for the governess to look through the window and frighten Mrs Grose exactly as James describes: 'She runs out and looks through the window as he had done as Mrs Grose enters' (I. 5). The definitive version of the libretto and the vocal score reverse these events: 'Mrs Grose enters as the governess rushes back into the room' (vocal score, p. 48).

11 This criticism seems to suggest that Mr Mason was imperfectly acquainted with the sequence of events in James's Chapter 11.

12 A minor discrepancy between the book and the libretto is that Quint enters Mrs Piper's scene at an earlier stage of the dialogue. In James, the governess sees Quint at the point at which she asks Miles if he stole her letter (p. 116).

13 See Donald Mitchell, 'Britten's Revisionary Practice: practical and creative', *Tempo*, 66–7 (1963), pp. 15–22.

3. Benjamin Britten's *The Turn of the Screw*: the music

1 This is bound in one volume, British Library Additional Manuscript 60602, on permanent loan to the Britten–Pears Library at Aldeburgh.

2 Benjamin Britten, *The Turn of the Screw*, Op. 54, an opera in a prologue and two acts. Libretto by Myfanwy Piper after the short story by Henry James. Vocal score by Imogen Holst. London, Boosey & Hawkes, 1955

3 Imogen Holst, *Britten*, The Great Composers series (London, 3rd ed, 1980), p. 55

4 Piper in Herbert (ed.), pp. 10–11

5 Basil Coleman (b. 1916), who produced *The Turn of the Screw* for the première at the Fenice theatre, Venice, on 14 September 1954

6 Fawley Bottom Farmhouse, near Henley-on-Thames, home of John and Myfanwy Piper since 1937

7 Piper in Herbert (ed.), p. 11. The 'gentle make-believe' turned out to be far more sinister in its effect in this scene.

8 The manuscript full score is bound in two volumes, British Library Additional Manuscript 60603/4, on permanent loan to the Britten–Pears Library at Aldeburgh.

9 Holst, *Britten*, p. 55

10 Britten, as quoted by Piper in Herbert (ed.), p. 11

11 Rehearsal figure numbers refer to the vocal score published by Boosey & Hawkes.

12 Holst, *Britten*, p. 56

13 See Mitchell, 'Britten's Revisionary Practice', pp. 15–22.

14 *Ibid.* p. 21

15 Peter Evans points out that the treatment of the theme in Variation IX utilises the principle of change-ringing: Peter Evans, *The Music of Benjamin Britten* (London, 1979), p. 212.

16 For example Mitchell, 'Britten's Revisionary Practice', pp. 18–22; Evans, *The Music of Benjamin Britten*, pp. 203–22

17 For example in a criticism of the first performance by Colin Mason: 'What is. . . important about the twelve-note row is that its sequence of rising fourths allow Britten to establish and preserve classical tonality in the work.' (*Guardian*, 15 September 1954, p. 5)

18 Britten quoted in Christopher Headington, *Britten* (London, 1981), p. 120

19 Erwin Stein, '*The Turn of the Screw* and its Musical Idiom', *Tempo*, 34 (1955), p. 6

20 For a concise account of all the variations the reader is referred to Evans, *The Music of Benjamin Britten*, pp. 210–13.

21 Though Britten's original attempt to orient Variation III in B minor and the 'Malo' song in E minor (see above, pp. 67 and 68) must tend to shake the reader's faith in the inevitability of the tonal organisation of the opera!

22 'I can't think wherever she must have picked up – ' 'The appalling language she applied to me? I can, then!' I broke in with a laugh that was doubtless significant enough.
It only, in truth, left my friend still more grave. 'Well, perhaps I ought to also – since I've heard some of it before!' (James, p. 107)

23 Examples of sets of variations, many involving passacaglia techniques, include: *A Boy was Born*, op. 3, 1933; *Variations on a Theme of Frank Bridge*, op. 10, 1937; Finale of Violin Concerto, op. 15, 1939; 'Lyke-wake Dirge' (from *Serenade for Tenor, Horn and Strings*, op. 31) 1943; 'Death be not proud' (from *The Holy Sonnets of John Donne*, op. 35) 1945; Chaconny from String Quartet No. 2, op. 36, 1945; *The Young Person's Guide to the Orchestra*, op. 34, 1946; *Lachrymae* for viola and piano, op. 48, 1950 etc.

24 See Chapter 2, p. 60.

25 It is the most abrupt ending of all Britten's operas and faithfully mirrors the equally terse conclusion in James.

26 In a sense, of course (at least in James), Quint *wins* – for Miles, in dying, presumably joins him and Miss Jessel in the World of Shades. But this is only one of the innumerable ambiguities with which *The Turn of the Screw* is fraught.

27 It is heard for the first time when the governess receives the letter advising her that Miles has been dismissed his school; but at this point we have yet to meet Quint and therefore cannot associate this tone colour specifically with him (see above, p. 87).

28 See Donald Mitchell, 'What do we know about Britten now?' in *The Britten Companion*, ed. C. Palmer (London, 1984), pp. 39–45, and 'Catching on to the Technique in Pagoda-land', *ibid.*, pp. 205–7. In this chapter Dr Mitchell discusses two important but little-noted influences on Britten, that of Russian music as well as of the Orient. In fact the two

are not so far removed, either geographically or musically, and it is significant that Russian composers themselves, with their love of bright colours, simple melodies and strong rhythms, their inclination towards repetition-with-modification and variation as opposed to symphonic development and disquisition – all childlike characteristics of Britten the child-man-composer as well – have often oriented themselves orientally. Exotic colorations in Britten's favourite Russian composer Tchaikovsky (whose ballets were the model for *The Prince of the Pagodas* not only orchestration-wise but in the perfection of their small forms) are almost a commonplace: particularly intriguing sound effects are to be heard in the scherzo of the Fourth Symphony and in the remarkable Second Orchestral Suite. Prokofiev's far-flinging orchestral imagination, as revealed not only in *Romeo and Juliet* but also in the amazing *Cantata for the Twentieth Anniversary of the Revolution* and the *Ode to the End of the War*, is no less flagrantly anti-academic. [*The Britten Companion* was published too late for any contributor to the present volume, other than Christopher Palmer, to have read.]

29 McPhee's inscription on the copy of the *Balinese Ceremonial Music* he gave Britten in April 1940 reads: 'To Ben – hoping he'll find something in the music, after all.' As Dr Mitchell comments, 'scarcely an inscription to a convert' (*The Britten Companion*, p. 40).

30 The relationship between the *Balinese Ceremonial Music* and this bell-sequence in *Grimes* was first discovered by Bayan Northcott and is described in detail by David Matthews in his analysis of Act II in the Cambridge Opera Handbook on *Peter Grimes*, ed. Philip Brett (Cambridge, 1983), pp. 122–4.

31 'Turning the Screw' in *The Britten Companion*, p. 149. [However, see above, p. 46, for an inspiration nearer home. P. H.]

32 The conventionally celestial or supernatural overtones of the celesta are unconventionally used by Bax in his *Garden of Fand* where the celesta solo which precedes Fand's Song of Immortal Love almost certainly represents the silver apple branch in Celtic mythology, the passport to enter the other world before the hour appointed by death, whose music was so soothing that mortals who heard it forgot all troubles. (See Lewis Foreman, *Bax, a Composer and His Times* (London, 1983), p. 357.) But for Britten there seems generally to have been something rather creepy, or at least ambivalent, about the celesta, for apart from in Act I of *The Prince of the Pagodas* where it represents the magic casket which opens for Belle Rose of its own volition, it always seems to hint at some kind of homosexual rapport: Peter and his apprentice, Quint and Miles, Oberon and his changeling boy. However, there is a certain curious historical consistency in this inasmuch as the celesta made its first entry into music for the purpose of depicting a Sugar Plum Fairy (in, of course, Tchaikovsky's *Nutcracker*, which, as Donald Mitchell has pointed out (see note 28 above), was one of the models for *The Prince of the Pagodas*). Another orchestral score undoubtedly familiar to Britten was Mahler's Sixth Symphony, in the finale of which (as Donald Mitchell pointed out to me in conversation) the celesta is indubitably associated with the powers of darkness – it is an important constituent of that lurid light

which fitfully returns to envelop the landscape, and is the immediate – and solo – harbinger of the third and fatal hammer-stroke. In the Sixth Symphony Mahler used the celesta for the first time in the (and I mean 'the' in its general sense) symphony, though it is earlier to be heard in the 1900 Rückert song 'Ich atmet' einen linden Duft' (see p. 120).

33 See Mitchell, 'Catching on to the Technique in Pagoda-land', *The Britten Companion*, p. 208 n. 22.

34 I am indebted to Jill Burrows for first drawing my attention to the intrinsic significance of the names in James's story. The connotations of 'Mrs Grose' and 'Flora' are obvious enough; but Miles (= 'soldier') surely suggests a capacity for unlimited development (are not Quint's long-miles-long melismata on the name in themselves a kind of musical reflection of this?) and 'Miss Jessel' (note the snake-like hissing sibilants) has appropriately predatory connotations, a 'jess' being a short strap round the leg of a hawk. By contrast the soft liquidity of the very sound of 'Quint' is seductive. And what are we to make of the fact that the only characters in the story who are *not* named are the governess and the guardian – linked not only by alliteration but in their common assumption of power over the fates of the children? Are the two in league together – is *theirs* the plot to destroy the children, or at least Miles, the object of most people's interest? ('Together we have destroyed him' – but who are 'we' and who is 'him'?)

[Comment by the editor: These names have, besides, a more basic significance. By 'Miles' and 'Flora', James must surely have intended to represent simply 'M' and 'F', pointing up the inescapably sexual roles they have to play. Similarly it cannot be coincidental that the Guardian, Governess and Mrs Grose are *all three* linked alliteratively. With what implication? Perhaps as 'grown-ups' – underlining the antithesis between the child's world and the adult's which Jonathan Miller's production suggests as the mainspring of the action (see Chapter 4, p. 148). I have less confidence in interpreting any special significance in J and Q. Possibly these were selected as remote, even exotic initials, certainly one degree removed from the frequency of Ms, Fs and Gs. This very simple interpretation in no way adjudicates between the alternative readings of the story and is, to me, the more convincing because of its noncommittal symbolism. In terms of sound, I cannot myself find a 'soft liquidity' in the name 'Quint'; for me it exactly matches the precise, percussive timbre of the celesta. P. H.]

35 Arthur Machen in his short story *The White People* makes some interesting comments on the affinity between sorcery and sanctity, between black and white, which pertinently apply to *The Turn of the Screw*: each, he claims, is an ecstasy, a withdrawal from the common life. The one is the infernal miracle, the other the supernal. People make the mistake of confining the spiritual world to the supremely good; but the supremely wicked, necessarily, have their portion in it. The connexion between Sin with the capital letter and actions commonly branded as sinful is no greater than that between the ABC and fine literature:

Evil in its essence is a lonely thing, a passion of the solitary, individual soul. It is wholly positive – but on the wrong side. It is the turning of everything upside-down, an attempt to penetrate into another and higher sphere in a forbidden manner, in a profoundly unnatural way. Holiness works on lines that *were* natural once; it is an effort to recover the ecstasy that was before the Fall. But sin is an effort to gain the ecstasy and the knowledge that pertains alone to angels, and in making this effort man – whosoever he is, whatever age he is, whatever his outward earthly demeanour – becomes a demon. He repeats the Fall. Sometimes we – more likely women, children, even animals – experience horror in the mere presence of evil. But with most of us convention and civilisation and education have blinded and deafened and obscured the natural reason so that we are as incapable of appreciating true wickedness as we are of true holiness or genius.

The relevance of these issues not merely to *The Turn of the Screw* but to the whole of Britten's life and work scarcely needs emphasising. A good description of the music of the *Screw* (at least as I am trying to present it) would be as 'wholly positive – but on the wrong side'. The Great Sinner of Machen's *White People* is a little girl who records her own attempts to attain to a forbidden ecstasy in a journal whose simple, childlike, unselfconscious manner throws into the greatest possible relief its horror of matter. The protagonist of another Machen story, *The Bright Boy*, is a bright and handsome little boy, no more in appearance than nine or ten but in reality, when finally brought to book, between fifty and sixty at least, and the perpetrator of a years-long, world-wide catalogue of evil and debauch.

36 See Donald Mitchell, 'A Billy Budd Notebook', *Opera News* (New York) 31 March 1979, p. 13.

37 Despite the wealth of Mahlerian reference, the model for this archetypal Britten passage in *Bunyan* and its many derivations in later works (for example *A Midsummer Night's Dream*) was more probably, I suggest, the *Andante tranquillo* central episode of Bridge's *Enter Spring*, a work which, Britten himself acknowledged, made an enormous impression on him when he first heard it as a schoolboy.

38 Not, as would have been the obvious way to do it, in the stopped horn, which is tethered throughout to the melodic line in support of the children (Britten is concerned throughout the score to give them as much orchestral help and guidance as he possibly can) but through an extraordinary combination of *pizzicato* strings (particularly the resonant open As and Es of the violins which Britten had already used to good effect, though *arco*, in the governess's coach-music) and converging flute and bassoon figures, pointed by side-drum. The ear may be deceived into thinking that the stopped horn *is* involved – but there is often an element of Ravel-like illusion about Britten's orchestral procedures. Much could be said about the affinities between Ravel and Britten, both in their different ways child-composers; *L'Enfant et les sortilèges* could almost have been written by Britten, and indeed the onomatopoeic bird-noises already mentioned could well originate in the night-garden scene in that opera, rather than in Bartók.

39 There is even an incidental extra-dramatic link between Quint and Miles here inasmuch as the 'real' pianist in the pit plays of course both piano *and* celesta.

40 Eric Walter White, *Benjamin Britten: his Life and Operas* (London, 1970), pp. 125–6.

41 *The Music of Benjamin Britten*, p. 203. Professor Evans writes convincingly of Britten's reflecting in *The Turn of the Screw* that side of Mahler 'racked by a conflict between youthful aspirations and self-consuming irony', of a creator whose music could hint at 'the emotional subtleties and undertones which, before and (if decreasingly) after Freud, make their effect chiefly at a subconscious level'. Professor Evans sees in the Britten–James music the same ambiguities, the 'innocence touched with wordly wisdom', the 'terror mounting below high spirits', that are of the essence of Mahler's art.

42 It is therefore not quite fair to accord Britten exclusive credit for 'rediscovering' Purcell any more than to hail him as virtually the first complete 'professional' in English music. The professionalism which stood him in such good stead was fostered in him by Bridge, who in turn had inherited it from his own teacher, Stanford. Britten would no doubt have had little more time for Stanford than for Parry; yet it is impossible to be acquainted with some of Parry's songs and choral works without realising that he, too, had some feeling for Purcellian principles of prosody. Britten's unfailing excellence in his choice of texts is another part of Parry's legacy, and the anthology concept which Britten made memorably his own has a precedent in certain works of Bliss – *Morning Heroes*, *Pastoral* and *Serenade* – all composed in the 1920s. To point out which is in no way to diminish Britten's achievement, simply to affirm his links with an older tradition of British music against other aspects of which he consciously rebelled.

43 Quint's *Sprechgesang* here is, of course, another clear anticipation of the Tempter's music in *The Prodigal Son*.

4. *The Turn of the Screw* in the theatre

The articles by Franco Abbiati, Louis Barcata and Riccardo Malipiero quoted in this chapter have been translated by Martin Ennis.

1 Letter from Mrs Piper to the author, 22 February 1982

2 Paul Griffiths has suggested that the more successfully an adult Flora captures the 'mannerisms and demeanour' of an eight-year-old, the less credible the impersonation is: 'the effort is all too clear. . . that embarrassing enactment of little-girl sweetness and temper vitiates the production as music theatre' (*The Times*, 10 September 1976, p. 9). Flora either *is* 'sweet' or is determinedly *feigning* sweetness. To interpose another layer of acting, of an adult striving for sweetness, threatens the integrity of Flora's characterisation.

3 For example Louis Barcata in the *Hamburger Fremdenblatt*, 18 September 1954 and Franco Abbiati in the *Corriere della sera*, 15 September 1954

4 As recently as 1976, Desmond Shawe-Taylor wrote of the 'fashionable notion that the two ghosts may be only figments of the Governess's overheated imagination. I cannot see that either Mrs Piper's libretto or James's tale lends any colour to such a theory' (*Sunday Times*, 31 October 1976, p. 37).

5 'As is his wont Britten has again not chosen a salubrious subject of

immediate appeal' (21 September 1955, p. 3). 'What many people will ask is how the opera fares in repeated hearings. The short answer is that what are at first *coups de théâtre* contrived by Mrs Piper in a clever libretto remain turns of the dramatic screw. On a longer consideration the question comes back to another one: is Henry James's tale fit matter for opera?' (27 September 1956, p. 5). 'Britten's opera. . . is, like its literary original, a deeply disturbing document that is also a major creative achievement. If it were not so well done we could wish it had never been done' (13 October 1962, p. 4).

6   The opera had already been *heard* in Britain: the première was broadcast live on the Third Programme.

7   Letter from Geoffrey Connor to the author, 6 December 1983

Bibliography

Archibald, W. *The Innocents*, New York, 1950

Blyth, A. *Remembering Britten*, London, 1981

Brown, D. 'Stimulus and Form in Britten's Works', *Music and Letters*, 39 (1958)

Culshaw, J. 'Ben: A Tribute to Benjamin Britten', *The Gramophone*, February 1977

Edel, L. *The Life of Henry James*, Harmondsworth, 1977

Evans, P. *The Music of Benjamin Britten*, London, 1979
'Britten', *The New Grove*, London, 1981
'Sonata Structures in Early Britten', *Tempo*, 82 (1967)
'Britten's Fourth Creative Decade', *Tempo* 106 (1973)

Gishford, A. (ed.) *Tribute to Benjamin Brittén on his Fiftieth Birthday*, London, 1963

Headington, C. *Britten*, London, 1981

Herbert, D. (ed.) *The Operas of Benjamin Britten*, London, 1979

Holst, I. *Britten*, The Great Composers series, London, 3rd edn, 1980
'Working for Benjamin Britten', *Musical Times*, 118 (1977)

Hurd, M. *Benjamin Britten*, London, 1966

Keller, H. 'Death of a genius', *Spectator*, 15 January 1977

Kennedy, M. *Britten*, London, 1981

Kobbé, ed. The Earl of Harewood *The Complete Opera Book*, London, 1976

Lindler, H. *Benjamin Britten: das Opernwerk*, Bonn, 1955

Lubbock, P. (ed.) *The Letters of Henry James*, London, 1920

Martin, J. Purdon. 'A Neurologist's View', *English National Opera programme booklet*, 6 November 1979

Matthiessen, F. O. & Murdock, K. B. (eds.) *The Notebooks of Henry James*, New York, 1947

Mitchell, D. 'Britten's Revisionary Practice: practical and creative', *Tempo*, 66-7 (1963)

Mitchell, D. & Evans, J. *Benjamin Britten, 1913-1976: Pictures from a Life*, London, 1978

Palmer, C. (ed.) *The Britten Companion*, London, 1984: see pp. 153f n. 28

Routh, F. 'Benjamin Britten' in *Contemporary British Music*, London, 1972

Schafer, M. *British Composers in Interview*, London, 1963

Stein, E. '*The Turn of the Screw* and its Musical Idiom', *Tempo*, 34 (1955)

Tempo, Britten fiftieth birthday issue, 66–7 (1963)
Britten sixtieth birthday issue, 106 (1973)
Tippett, M. *Music of the Angels*, London, 1980
White, E. W. *Benjamin Britten: a Sketch of his Life and Works*, London, 1948, revised 1954
Benjamin Britten: his Life and Operas, London, 1970
Whittall, A. *The Music of Britten and Tippett*, Cambridge, 1982
'Benjamin Britten', *Music Review*, 23 (1962)
Young, P. *Benjamin Britten*, London, 1966

Reviews of the first performance consulted in connexion with Chapter 4

Aux écoutes (Paris, 1 October 1954)
Avanti (Milan, 15 September 1954)
L'avvenire d'Italia (Bologna, 15 September 1954)
Badische neueste Nachrichten (Karlsruhe, 25 September 1954)
Les Beaux Arts (Brussels, 1 October 1954)
Corriere della sera (Milan, 15 September 1954)
The Daily Telegraph (London, 15 September 1954)
L'Express (Paris, 25 September 1954)
Il giornale (Naples, 15 September 1954)
The Guardian (Manchester, 15 September 1954)
Hamburger Fremdenblatt (Hamburg, 18 September 1954)
La Libre Belgique (Brussels, 27 September 1954)
Le Monde (Paris, 28 September 1954)
New York Herald Tribune (New York, 26 September 1954)
La nuova stampa (Turin, 15 September 1954)
The Observer (London, 19 September 1954)
Il popolo (Milan, 15 September 1954)
The Sunday Times (London, 19 September 1954)
Time (New York, 27 September 1954)
The Times (London, 15 September 1954 and 16 September 1954)

Discography

Only two recordings are available at time of writing:

1955   Members of English Opera Group conducted by Britten;
Vyvyan, Pears, Mandikian, Cross, Dyer, Hemmings
             Decca Ace of Diamonds mono
             GOM 560–1 (two records)

1984   Members of Covent Garden Orchestra conducted by Colin Davis;
Donath, Tear, Harper, June, Watson, Ginn
             Philips 410 426–1 (two records);
             410 426–4 (cassette)

Index

Act 1.   Prologue

    1. Journey

    2. Welcome.

    3. Letter — Lavender's Blue

    4. Tower

    5. Window.

    6. Lesson — Malo
    ——————————————

    7. The Lake

    8. At Night

Act 2. 1. Colloquy

    2. The Bell, ⟶ decides to leave

    3. Miss Jessel ⟶ writes letter.

    4. The Bedroom

    5. Quint ⟶ steals the letter

    6. Piano.

    7. Flora

    8. Miles.

post.

1.　　　2　　　3　　　4　　　5　　　6　　　7.

MA
abbey
(−1/24)

$\frac{32}{T}$ 513ks   BBK.

?

8.　　　9

- vermin
- study Italian
- write a play

Fractio of a dramatry
in an opera

Screw
claustrophobia
Watch image

• Why did the ghosts come?
 └ what do they want?

• 라파 [Korean] 에게 ... "가 죽...보5 fact.
 └ who 죽 who? — a mad woman?
                    or a medium?
              exorcist

Victorian - Georgian
         Regency

[Korean]. different story
          to different people
        → [Korean].

ambiguity?
 appen!
 [Korean]

[Korean]   Window / Tower
verse + prose   Both

Printed in Great Britain
by Amazon